Healthy Friendships

Recent Titles in
Q&A Health Guides

Sexually Transmitted Diseases: Your Questions Answered
Paul Quinn

Mindfulness and Meditation: Your Questions Answered
Blaise Aguirre

Anxiety and Panic Attacks: Your Questions Answered
Daniel Zwillenberg

Substance Abuse: Your Questions Answered
Romeo Vitelli

Eating Disorders: Your Questions Answered
Justine J. Reel

Food Allergies and Sensitivities: Your Questions Answered
Alice C. Richer

Obesity: Your Questions Answered
Christine L. B. Selby

Birth Control: Your Questions Answered
Paul Quinn

Therapy and Counseling: Your Questions Answered
Christine L. B. Selby

Depression: Your Questions Answered
Romeo Vitelli

Food Labels: Your Questions Answered
Barbara A. Brehm

Smoking: Your Questions Answered
Stacy Mintzer Herlihy

Grief and Loss: Your Questions Answered
Louis Kuykendall Jr.

Teen Stress: Your Questions Answered
Nicole Neda Zamanzadeh and Tamara D. Afifi

HEALTHY FRIENDSHIPS

Your Questions Answered

Lauren Holleb

Q&A Health Guides

GREENWOOD

An Imprint of ABC-CLIO, LLC

Santa Barbara, California • Denver, Colorado

Library of Congress Cataloging-in-Publication Data

Names: Holleb, Lauren, author.
Title: Healthy friendships : your questions answered / Lauren Holleb.
Description: Santa Barbara, California : Greenwood, [2021] | Series: Q&A
  health guides | Includes bibliographical references and index.
Identifiers: LCCN 2020033470 (print) | LCCN 2020033471 (ebook) | ISBN
  9781440867354 (hardcover ; alk. paper) | ISBN 9781440867361 (ebook)
Subjects: LCSH: Friendship in adolescence—Juvenile literature. |
  Friendship—Juvenile literature.
Classification: LCC BF724.3.F64 H65 2021 (print) | LCC BF724.3.F64
  (ebook) | DDC 177/.62—dc23
LC record available at https://lccn.loc.gov/2020033470
LC ebook record available at https://lccn.loc.gov/2020033471

ISBN: 978-1-4408-6735-4 (print)
        978-1-4408-6736-1 (ebook)

25 24 23 22 21 1 2 3 4 5

This book is also available as an eBook.

Greenwood
An Imprint of ABC-CLIO, LLC

ABC-CLIO, LLC
147 Castilian Drive
Santa Barbara, California 93117
www.abc-clio.com

This book is printed on acid-free paper ∞

Manufactured in the United States of America

For E & E . . . May you always have a true friend in one another.

Contents

Series Foreword

All of us have questions about our health. Is this normal? Should I be doing something differently? Whom should I talk to about my concerns? And our modern world is full of answers. Thanks to the Internet, there's a wealth of information at our fingertips, from forums where people can share their personal experiences to Wikipedia articles to the full text of medical studies. But finding the right information can be an intimidating and difficult task—some sources are written at too high a level, others have been oversimplified, while still others are heavily biased or simply inaccurate.

Q&A Health Guides address the needs of readers who want accurate, concise answers to their health questions, authored by reputable and objective experts, and written in clear and easy-to-understand language. This series focuses on the topics that matter most to young adult readers, including various aspects of physical and emotional well-being as well as other components of a healthy lifestyle. These guides will also serve as a valuable tool for parents, school counselors, and others who may need to answer teens' health questions.

All books in the series follow the same format to make finding information quick and easy. Each volume begins with an essay on health literacy and why it is so important when it comes to gathering and evaluating health information. Next, the top five myths and misconceptions that surround the topic are dispelled. The heart of each guide is a collection of questions and answers, organized thematically. A selection of five case studies provides real-world examples to illuminate key concepts. Rounding out each volume are a directory of resources, glossary, and index.

It is our hope that the books in this series will not only provide valuable information but will also help guide readers toward a lifetime of healthy decision making.

Acknowledgments

I would like to thank several people who helped make this book possible. First and foremost, I would like to thank my family: my husband, Tim, and my son and daughter, Everett and Ella. Their support allowed me the time and energy needed to complete this project, and their love helps make everything I do possible. I would also like to thank my editor, Maxine Taylor, first, for offering me this project, but even more so for her unwavering guidance, support, invaluable feedback, and patience. She has been a pleasure to work with on this book. Thank you to Cindy Erdley. You believed in my potential, all those years ago, and you have provided me with invaluable mentorship. For that, I am eternally grateful. Next, I would like to thank my students for providing input and feedback on content, and Aaron Withers for his research support. I would also like to thank my colleagues (Rachelle Smith and Christine Selby) at Husson University, who paved the way with their own book projects and for their patience as I worked on mine. Finally, I would like to thank all of my family and friends. You have shown me the true meaning and value of friendship, and I would not be where I am today without your guidance and support.

Introduction

There is a lot of focus in the popular media on negative aspects of friendship, such as bullying. However, there is so much positive that friendship can offer us as well. Unfortunately, the benefits that friendship affords us in life seem to receive much less attention. Scientific research, however, has focused on helping us to better understand just what it is that friendship provides for us and how those who are lacking in friendship might be negatively impacted. This research has demonstrated that friendship has a clear positive impact on our socio-emotional well-being and can serve a protective function for those who may be at risk. Friendship is something that all of us encounter in our lives. As a college professor and licensed psychologist working with children and adolescents, I get asked many questions about friendship. This book covers many of those questions.

The purpose of this book is to shed light on research via answers to common questions that people have about friendship and provide some practical advice for common problems encountered over the course of a friendship. The book begins by addressing several common myths associated with friendship. The question-and-answer portion of the book is divided into the following categories: general information and definitions, different and changing friendships, the impact of friendship on what to do as a friend, current trends in friendship, and research. The book concludes with several case vignettes designed to illustrate common scenarios associated with friendship. The book also includes a glossary of terms and a directory of resources.

I hope this book encourages you to think about friendship in new ways you had not previously considered and provides you with practical information that will be useful to you as you navigate friendships throughout your life.

Guide to Health Literacy

On her 13th birthday, Samantha was diagnosed with type 2 diabetes. She consulted her mom and her aunt, both of whom also have type 2 diabetes, and decided to go with their strategy of managing diabetes by taking insulin. As a result of participating in an after-school program at her middle school that focused on health literacy, she learned that she can help manage the level of glucose in her bloodstream by counting her carbohydrate intake, following a diabetic diet, and exercising regularly. But, what exactly should she do? How does she keep track of her carbohydrate intake? What is a diabetic diet? How long should she exercise and what type of exercise should she do? Samantha is a visual learner, so she turned to her favorite source of media, YouTube, to answer these questions. She found videos from individuals around the world sharing their experiences and tips, doctors (or at least people who have "Dr." in their YouTube channel names), government agencies such as the National Institutes of Health, and even video clips from cat lovers who have cats with diabetes. With guidance from the librarian and the health and science teachers at her school, she assessed the credibility of the information in these videos and even compared their suggestions to some of the print resources that she was able to find at her school library. Now, she knows exactly how to count her carbohydrate level, how to prepare and follow a diabetic diet, and how much (and what) exercise is needed daily. She intends to share her findings with her mom and her aunt, and now she wants to create a chart that summarizes what she has learned that she can share with her doctor.

Samantha's experience is not unique. She represents a shift in our society; an individual no longer views himself or herself as a passive recipient of medical care but as an active mediator of his or her own health. However, in this era when any individual can post his or her opinions and experiences with a particular health condition online with just a few clicks or publish a memoir, it is vital that people know how to assess the credibility of health information. Gone are the days when "publishing" health information required intense vetting. The health information landscape is highly saturated, and people have innumerable sources where they can find information about practically any health topic. The sources (whether print, online, or a person) that an individual consults for health information are crucial because the accuracy and trustworthiness of the information can potentially affect his or her overall health. The ability to find, select, assess, and use health information constitutes a type of literacy—health literacy—that everyone must possess.

THE DEFINITION AND PHASES OF HEALTH LITERACY

One of the most popular definitions for health literacy comes from Ratzan and Parker (2000), who describe health literacy as "the degree to which individuals have the capacity to obtain, process, and understand basic health information and services needed to make appropriate health decisions." Recent research has extrapolated health literacy into health literacy bits, further shedding light on the multiple phases and literacy practices that are embedded within the multifaceted concept of health literacy. Although this research has focused primarily on online health information seeking, these health literacy bits are needed to successfully navigate both print and online sources. There are six phases of health information seeking: (1) Information Need Identification and Question Formulation, (2) Information Search, (3) Information Comprehension, (4) Information Assessment, (5) Information Management, and (6) Information Use.

The first phase is the *information need identification and question formulation phase*. In this phase, one needs to be able to develop and refine a range of questions to frame one's search and understand relevant health terms. In the second phase, *information search*, one has to possess appropriate searching skills, such as using proper keywords and correct spelling in search terms, especially when using search engines and databases. It is also crucial to understand how search engines work (i.e., how search results are derived, what the order of the search results means, how to use the snippets that are provided in the search results list to select websites, and how to determine which listings are ads on a search engine results page). One also has to limit reliance on surface characteristics, such as the design of a website or a book (a website or book that appears to have a lot of information or looks aesthetically pleasant does not necessarily mean it has good information) and language used (a website or book that utilizes jargon, the keywords that one used to conduct the search, or the word "information" does not necessarily indicate it will have good information). The next phase is *information comprehension*, whereby one needs to have the ability to read, comprehend, and recall the information (including textual, numerical, and visual content) one has located from the books and/or online resources.

To assess the credibility of health information (*information assessment* phase), one needs to be able to evaluate information for accuracy, evaluate how current the information is (e.g., when a website was last updated or when a book was published), and evaluate the creators of the source—for example, examine site sponsors or type of sites (.com, .gov, .edu, or .org) or the author of a book (practicing doctor, a celebrity doctor, a patient of a specific disease, etc.) to determine the believability of the person/organization providing the information. Such credibility perceptions tend to become generalized, so they must be frequently reexamined (e.g., the belief that a specific news agency always has credible health information needs continuous vetting). One also needs to evaluate the credibility of the medium (e.g., television, Internet, radio, social media, and book) and evaluate—not just accept without questioning—others' claims regarding the validity of a site, book, or other specific source of information. At this stage, one has to "make sense of information gathered from diverse sources by identifying misconceptions, main and supporting ideas, conflicting information, point of view, and biases" (American Association of School Librarians [AASL], 2009, p. 13) and conclude which sources/information are valid and accurate by using conscious strategies rather than simply using intuitive judgments or "rules of thumb." This phase is the most challenging segment of health information seeking and serves as a determinant of success (or lack thereof) in the information-seeking process. The following section on Sources of Health Information further explains this phase.

The fifth phase is *information management*, whereby one has to organize information that has been gathered in some manner to ensure easy retrieval and use in the future. The last phase is *information use*, in which one will synthesize information found across various resources, draw conclusions, and locate the answer to his or her original question and/or the content that fulfills the information need. This phase also often involves implementation, such as using the information to solve a health problem; make health-related decisions; identify and engage in behaviors that will help a person to avoid health risks; share the health information found with family members and friends who may benefit from it; and advocate more broadly for personal, family, or community health.

THE IMPORTANCE OF HEALTH LITERACY

The conception of health has moved from a passive view (someone is either well or ill) to one that is more active and process based (someone is working toward preventing or managing disease). Hence, the dominant focus has shifted from doctors and treatments to patients and prevention, resulting in the need to strengthen our ability and confidence (as patients and consumers of health care) to look for, assess, understand, manage, share, adapt, and use health-related information. An individual's health literacy level has been found to predict his or her health status better than age, race, educational attainment, employment status, and income level (National Network of Libraries of Medicine, 2013). Greater health literacy also enables individuals to better communicate with health care providers such as doctors, nutritionists, and therapists, as they can pose more relevant, informed, and useful questions to health care providers. Another added advantage of greater health literacy is better information-seeking skills, not only for health but also in other domains, such as completing assignments for school.

SOURCES OF HEALTH INFORMATION: THE GOOD, THE BAD, AND THE IN-BETWEEN

For generations, doctors, nurses, nutritionists, health coaches, and other health professionals have been the trusted sources of health information. Additionally, researchers have found that young adults, when they have health-related questions, typically turn to a family member who has had firsthand experience with a health condition because of their family member's close proximity and because of their past experience with, and trust in, this individual. Expertise should be a core consideration when consulting a person, website, or book for health information. The credentials and background of the person or author and conflicting interests of the author (and his or her organization) must be checked and validated to ensure the likely credibility of the health information they are conveying. While books often have implied credibility because of the peer-review process involved, self-publishing has challenged this credibility, so qualifications of book authors should also be verified. When it comes to health information, currency of the source must also be examined. When examining health information/studies presented, pay attention to the exhaustiveness of research methods utilized to offer recommendations or conclusions. Small and nondiverse sample size is often—but not always—an indication of reduced credibility. Studies that confuse correlation with causation is another potential issue to watch for. Information seekers must also pay attention to the sponsors of the research studies. For example, if a study is sponsored by manufacturers of drug Y and the study recommends that drug Y is the best treatment to manage or cure a disease, this may indicate a lack of objectivity on the part of the researchers.

The Internet is rapidly becoming one of the main sources of health information. Online forums, news agencies, personal blogs, social media sites, pharmacy sites, and celebrity "doctors" are all offering medical and health information targeted to various types of people in regard to all types of diseases and symptoms. There are professional journalists, citizen journalists, hoaxers, and people paid to write fake health news on various sites that may appear to have a legitimate domain name and may even have authors who claim to have professional credentials, such as an MD. All these sites *may* offer useful information or information that appears to be useful and relevant; however, much of the information may be debatable and may fall into gray areas that require readers to discern credibility, reliability, and biases.

While broad recognition and acceptance of certain media, institutions, and people often serve as the most popular determining factors to assess credibility of health information among young people, keep in mind that there are legitimate Internet sites, databases, and books that publish health information and serve as sources of health information for doctors, other health sites, and members of the public. For example, MedlinePlus (https://medlineplus.gov) has trusted sources on over 975 diseases and conditions and presents the information in easy-to-understand language.

The chart here presents factors to consider when assessing credibility of health information. However, keep in mind that these factors function only as a guide and require continuous updating to keep abreast with the changes in the landscape of health information, information sources, and technologies.

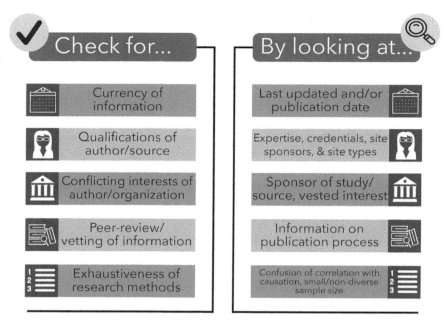

All images from flaticon.com

The chart can serve as a guide; however, approaching a librarian about how one can go about assessing the credibility of both print and online health information is far more effective than using generic checklist-type tools. While librarians are not health experts, they can apply and teach patrons strategies to determine the credibility of health information.

With the prevalence of fake sites and fake resources that appear to be legitimate, it is important to use the following health information assessment tips to verify health information that one has obtained (St. Jean et al., 2015, p. 151):

- **Don't assume you are right**: Even when you feel very sure about an answer, keep in mind that the answer may not be correct, and it is important to conduct (further) searches to validate the information.
- **Don't assume you are wrong**: You may actually have correct information, even if the information you encounter does not match—that is, you may be right and the resources that you have found may contain false information.
- **Take an open approach**: Maintain a critical stance by not including your preexisting beliefs as keywords (or letting them influence your

choice of keywords) in a search, as this may influence what it is possible to find out.

- **Verify, verify, and verify**: Information found, especially on the Internet, needs to be validated, no matter how the information appears on the site (i.e., regardless of the appearance of the site or the quantity of information that is included).

Health literacy comes with experience navigating health information. Professional sources of health information, such as doctors, health care providers, and health databases, are still the best, but one also has the power to search for health information and then verify it by consulting with these trusted sources and by using the health information assessment tips and guide shared previously.

Mega Subramaniam, PhD
Associate Professor, College of Information Studies,
University of Maryland

REFERENCES AND FURTHER READING

American Association of School Librarians (AASL). (2009). *Standards for the 21st-century learner in action.* Chicago, IL: American Association of School Librarians.

Hilligoss, B., & Rieh, S.-Y. (2008). Developing a unifying framework of credibility assessment: Construct, heuristics, and interaction in context. *Information Processing & Management, 44*(4), 1467–1484.

Kuhlthau, C. C. (1988). Developing a model of the library search process: Cognitive and affective aspects. *Reference Quarterly, 28*(2), 232–242.

National Network of Libraries of Medicine (NNLM). (2013). Health literacy. Bethesda, MD: National Network of Libraries of Medicine. Retrieved from nnlm.gov/outreach/consumer/hlthlit.html

Ratzan, S. C., & Parker, R. M. (2000). Introduction. In C. R. Selden, M. Zorn, S. C. Ratzan, & R. M. Parker (Eds.), *National Library of Medicine current bibliographies in medicine: Health literacy.* NLM Pub. No. CBM 2000-1. Bethesda, MD: National Institutes of Health, U.S. Department of Health and Human Services.

St. Jean, B., Taylor, N. G., Kodama, C., & Subramaniam, M. (February 2017). Assessing the health information source perceptions of tweens using card-sorting exercises. *Journal of Information Science.* Retrieved from http://journals.sagepub.com/doi/abs/10.1177/0165551516687728

St. Jean, B., Subramaniam, M., Taylor, N. G., Follman, R., Kodama, C., & Casciotti, D. (2015). The influence of positive hypothesis testing on youths' online health-related information seeking. *New Library World*, *116*(3/4), 136–154.

Subramaniam, M., St. Jean, B., Taylor, N. G., Kodama, C., Follman, R., & Casciotti, D. (2015). Bit by bit: Using design-based research to improve the health literacy of adolescents. *JMIR Research Protocols*, *4*(2), paper e62. Retrieved from http://www.ncbi.nlm.nih.gov/pmc/articles /PMC4464334/

Valenza, J. (2016, November 26). Truth, truthiness, and triangulation: A news literacy toolkit for a "post-truth" world [Web log]. Retrieved from http://blogs.slj.com/neverendingsearch/2016/11/26/truth-truthiness -triangulation-and-the-librarian-way-a-news-literacy-toolkit-for-a -post-truth-world/

Common Misconceptions about Friendship

1. GIRLS AND BOYS/WOMEN AND MEN CAN'T JUST BE FRIENDS

Some people assume that there always has to be romantic interest between adolescent girls and boys and men and women and that it's not possible to just be platonic friends. Although sometimes one or both individuals may be romantically interested in one another, this is definitely not always the case. It is certainly possible for boys and girls and men and women to be just friends. Someone of the opposite sex can be your friend in much the same way as someone of the same sex. A true friend spends time with you, doesn't gossip, isn't jealous, and doesn't pass judgment. According to research, college students enjoy opposite-sex friends as dinner companions and conversation partners and believe that they can help to boost self-esteem. They also use these friends to get information about the opposite sex; and like their friendship for social status, respect, and the sharing of resources. Both sexes also note some similar costs of opposite-sex friendship, including jealousy, confusion over the status of the relationship, love not being reciprocated, mean behaviors, and being less attractive to potential romantic partners because of the friendship. Men are more apt to see romantic potential and sex as a benefit, while women view this as a cost. In addition, women view their male friends paying for outings and providing them with physical protection as benefits, while men view these as costs. So, while it may be possible for boys and girls and men and women to be friends, the benefits of this friendship likely differ based on sex. For more information, see Question 11.

2. HAVING MORE FRIENDS IS ALWAYS BETTER

In contrast to what you might expect, having more friends is not always better. This is an area where quality is definitely more important than quantity. In fact, having even one high-quality reciprocated friendship (i.e., both people view one another as a friend) can be protective for your psychological well-being. Research has demonstrated that older adults are more selective than younger adults when picking their social connections. These smaller social circles have a higher proportion of meaningful relationships that support a feeling of social well-being. So, in this day and age of social media where more friends may always seem better, remember that the number of friends you have is far less important than the quality of these relationships. Question 6 explores what makes a high-quality friendship in more detail.

3. IF YOU'VE BEEN FRIENDS FOR A LONG TIME, YOU'LL BE FRIENDS FOREVER

We've all seen the necklaces that say "Best friends forever." There is an assumption that if you've been friends for a long time, you're going to be or should be friends forever. However, in truth, most friendships do not last a lifetime. The majority of friendships end at some point for varying reasons. Friends may drift apart due to changes in life (e.g., moving, a new job, getting married, having a child). Friendships might also end due to a lack of trust or simply drifting apart over time. However, there are many things that you can do to work to maintain strong friendships, and these will be discussed throughout this book. Question 28 examines why friends sometimes drift apart.

4. YOU HAVE TO BE POPULAR AND/OR ATTRACTIVE TO HAVE FRIENDS

Especially when we are younger, there is an assumption that we really want to be popular with our peer group and that this is the only way we'll have good friends. We may also think we have to look a certain way, be pretty or handsome, and be the best dressed to have friends. Contrary to popular belief, none of these things are necessary or needed to have friends. Adolescents who are not popular with their peers typically do have friends, and being attractive is not necessary to have friends. What is most important, though, is having a high-quality reciprocated friendship. Students who are popular with their peers may have access to a larger pool of potential friends and often show high levels of prosocial skills that may make it easier for them to make friends. Questions 2, 3, and 4 explore this concept in more detail.

5. TECHNOLOGY IS BAD FOR FRIENDSHIPS

Simply stating that technology is bad for friendships is not true. Rather, the relationship between technology and friendship is a complicated one. Technology can help us to stay connected with friends who are far away, remain in contact with our friends when we are unable to see them, and share things about our lives with a broader social network. In particular, research seems to show that for youth who are socially competent and have positive face-to-face peer connections, the Internet may have a positive impact. However, for adolescents and young adults who are already struggling socially, it seems that the Internet may in fact exacerbate their social difficulties rather than enhance their social lives. It does seem that for anyone spending too much time online, that it can contribute to having thoughts that others' lives are better than one's own and lead to unhappiness. Thus, it is definitely important to maintain face-to-face social relationships in addition to an online presence. For additional information on this topic, see Question 33.

QUESTIONS AND ANSWERS

General Information and Definitions

1. What is friendship?

It might seem like defining friendship would be a straightforward task. After all, we all know what friendship is, right? However, friendship has been defined in many different ways that have often been dictated by the discipline exploring the concept. Psychologists view friendship as a special kind of close relationship between two individuals. Given that friendship is nearly always defined as an interpersonal relationship between two individuals, this is often referred to as a "dyadic relationship." Friendship is frequently defined as an equal or "horizontal" relationship since both individuals are expected to be on the same or similar level. Since friendship is viewed as a "horizontal" relationship, it differs in important ways from other social relationships, such as parent-child relationships that are inherently "vertical" in nature, where expectations of each member differ and a parent is considered to be in charge. As such, an important hallmark of friendship is reciprocity or mutuality, meaning that "I consider you to be my friend, and you also consider me to be your friend." When people, regardless of age, are asked to describe a friend, they emphasize this point. Individuals mention that friends support one another and that give and take forms the basis of friendship. While there are aspects of friendship that change with age (see Questions 7 and 8), the essence of friendship, reciprocity, remains the same throughout the full life span.

Although developmental psychologists have studied friendship most extensively, sociologists and anthropologists have also explored friendship. Sociologists view the individual as playing an active role in their own socialization. Friendship is viewed within a broader social context, and sociologists often examine the impact of gender, race, and socioeconomic status on friendship. Friendships are viewed as symbolic interactions and routines learned from adult interactions that are repeated within these relationships. The sociological definition of friendship tends to be the most inclusive. Friends are typically viewed as the peers with whom an individual frequently interacts, and friends can include small groups rather than just dyads. Sociological research often asks an individual to indicate who their friends are, as they are most interested in the individual's own perception. In contrast, psychological research usually contains a check to ensure that friendship is reciprocated (see Question 35 to learn more about friendship research). Friendship has only been infrequently studied by anthropologists. Rather than trying to identify one definition of friendship, anthropologists define friendship by its emergence in particular social and cultural contexts. This allows for different understandings of what constitutes friendship across cultures, and it has enabled the examination of similarities and differences in friendship across cultures.

Importantly, relationships with friends differ significantly from relationships of those who are not friends. Friendships are characterized by greater positivity, including more smiling, talking, sharing, cooperating, and helping, than other relationships. Although conflict is just as likely to occur with friends, children and adolescents' conflict resolution with friends tends to be better than with their general peer group. They are more likely to negotiate and focus on maintaining the relationship rather than asserting power and standing their ground. Similarly, friendships tend to be more equal relationships as they have less competition and domination than nonfriend relationships. Finally, friends tend to be similar to one another in important ways. (However, it is possible to be friends with people who differ from you. See Question 13 to learn more about this.) Specifically, friends tend to be similar in age, race, attitudes toward school, and level of delinquency. This similarity between one another is called homophily, and friends tend to become even more similar to one another over the course of a friendship.

2. How does friendship differ from peer acceptance?

The quality and number of an individual's reciprocated friendships is related to but is distinct from peer group acceptance. Peer acceptance is the degree to which members of a particular peer group (e.g., class, grade, school) like the individual. Similarly, peer rejection is the degree to which members of a particular peer group dislike the individual. (See Question 36 for more information about how peer acceptance is studied in the research literature.) In contrast to friendship, peer acceptance is a unilateral construct since it only represents the feelings of others directed toward the individual, not how the individual him- or herself feels. It may be expected that adolescents and young adults who are well-liked by the peer group would be more likely to have friends; however, some youth who are popular do not have close friends, and some who are rejected by their peer group do have close friendships. In addition, the social skills required for peer acceptance (e.g., cooperation, getting along well with others) also promote friendships, but friendship also requires having common ground, a mutual liking, and commitment to reciprocity. Peer acceptance does tend to predict the number of reciprocated friendships an individual has. This may be because those who are more popular may have more opportunities to form friendships, and popularity may temporally precede forming friendships.

Peer status has been associated with different types of interaction, association, and reputation. From a young age, children have been found to interact more positively with peers who are well-liked by their classmates. In addition, children who are popular with their peers are more likely to interact with other popular children, and over time, these popular children become the focus of peer group interaction, serving as consistent companions. In contrast, when children are rejected by their peers, they tend not to develop a consistent group of companions and often wander from one playmate to another. Rejected children tend to demonstrate difficulty entering the peer group and often select younger children with whom to play. Unfortunately, once children are rejected by their peer group, they are likely to remain rejected over time, and this consistently holds during adolescence as well.

When the behavior of rejected children and adolescents is explored, it is found that they are a diverse group who tend to have more behavior problems and are often described as antisocial, withdrawn, overactive, and prone to emotional problems. Children and adolescents who are well-liked tend to be more socially competent and cooperative than those who are rejected by their peers. They demonstrate good communication skills, regulate their emotions effectively, and demonstrate sensitivity and empathy for others. Finally, research has consistently demonstrated that those who are rejected by their peers are at risk for several adjustment difficulties both now and in the future. Specifically, youth who are rejected by their peers are at risk for loneliness, victimization, mental health problems, antisocial behavior, and delinquency. They are also more likely to drop out of school.

The larger peer group structure also comprises cliques and crowds during adolescence. Adolescents typically have multiple friends and spend time with multiple peers who comprise cohesive groups, called peer cliques. Put simply, these are peers who hang around with one another. It is possible to belong to more than one peer network, and these networks can overlap. These peer groups are often formed based on common activities. Crowds become another important facet of the peer world during adolescence. Crowds are large reputation-based groups that are not based on affiliation and can contain many peer networks. Crowd members may or may not interact with one another. Members are tied to one another based on a label ascribed to the group, such as "jocks," "nerds," or "druggies." Crowd affiliation can be an important part of identity for adolescents, but by later adolescence, it can be viewed as interfering with self-expression and identity development.

3. So, if you're well-liked by the peer group, does that mean you have good friends?

Several researchers have examined the relationship between peer acceptance, friendship prevalence, and relationship quality. For instance, research has demonstrated that not all high-accepted children and adolescents have best friends and that not all children low in peer acceptance lacked best friendships. However, high-accepted and average-accepted youth were twice as likely as low-accepted youth to have a mutual best friend. In addition, low-accepted youth report qualitatively poorer friendships than high- and average-accepted individuals. For average- and high-accepted youth, there was high concordance between their own and their friend's report of friendship quality. However, there was little relationship between their own and their friend's report of friendship quality for low-accepted youth. In particular, this was found concerning the extent that they viewed the friendship as being close and fun. It is also important to look at the behavior of youth that contributes to whether or not they are well-liked by the peer group. Many rejected youth appear to be aggressive and/or socially withdrawn, but their friendships are not as well investigated.

Research has found that the majority of aggressive children and adolescents have a mutual best friendship and are as likely as socially well-adjusted children and adolescents to have mutual friends. However, aggression does seem to be negatively related to friendship stability. So, more aggressive youth tend to have more changes in their friendship partners over time. Aggressive children and adolescents also tend to have friends who are more confrontational and antisocial and have high levels of relational aggression (e.g., threatening friendship withdrawal) and high levels of exclusivity/jealousy within their friendships. For socially withdrawn youth, their friendships are viewed as lacking in fun, intimacy, helpfulness and guidance, and validation and caring. There is also some research evidence to suggest that socially withdrawn youth are more likely than their peers to be chronically friendless over time.

When researchers first attempted to make the distinction between peer acceptance and friendship, these constructs initially overlapped. When trying to parse them out, investigators found that the distinction between peer acceptance and friendship is meaningful. Results indicated that not all high-accepted children and adolescents had friends. Specifically, just under one-third of high-accepted youth did not have someone that they named as their very best friend. In contrast, many low-accepted children did have other children and adolescents whom they named as friends. High-accepted youth were twice as likely to have a very best friend than low-accepted youth. This disparity was particularly wide for low-accepted boys, with only one in five having a very best friend. Youth who did not have best friends were lonelier than those who did have best friends, regardless of their level of peer acceptance. Friendship quality and peer acceptance were found to contribute equally to the level of loneliness for children and adolescents. Low-accepted and high-accepted youth's friendships tended to differ with regard to quality as well. Specifically, low-accepted youth's friendships were lower in the important provisions of validation and caring, help and guidance, conflict resolution, and intimate exchange and higher in conflict and betrayal than those of high-accepted youth. Importantly, low-accepted children and adolescents showed the highest amount of variability in friendship quality of any of the peer status groups.

So, it seems that being popular may not be as important as having a good-quality friendship. But don't adolescents put a lot of emphasis on being popular? The emphasis put on popularity increases over the elementary school years and peaks in late middle school and early high school. In support of this, research has found that less than 10 percent of children in grades one through four consider popularity more important than friendship, but over a quarter of fifth through eighth graders and one-third of ninth through twelfth graders did. Other research has found that early and middle adolescents generally place more emphasis on conforming and being part of a popular group than do younger or older children.

It may seem like being popular during adolescence is the ultimate goal, but is it actually even good for you? Friendships really are more important than popularity during adolescence. Specifically, close friendships during adolescence have been associated with an increase in self-worth and a decrease in anxiety and depressive symptoms in early adulthood. It seems that having a good-quality friendship or friendships during adolescence is definitely more important than being popular. Close friendships during adolescence were really predictive of mental health from age 15 to 25. As such, it is likely important for adolescents to focus more on their friendships and worry less about how well -liked they are by their overall peer group, in general.

4. What are social skills, and how are they important to friendship?

Although researchers have generally agreed on what problematic social behavior looks like, there has been less agreement about what socially competent behavior entails. However, most researchers agree that effectiveness in social interaction is a central component of social competence. From there, some researchers have focused on a specific set of social skills, sociometric status (how well-liked an individual is by the peer group), relationships, or functional outcomes. Those who use a social skills-based definition employ behavior checklists to identify socially competent children and adolescents. Sometimes this list of social skills is based on theory, while other times it is constructed based on social values. Specifically, social skills that are valued by peers and teachers are included. Finally, other researchers employing the social skills approach to defining social competence use a competence correlates strategy. In this approach, behaviors are selected based upon their correlation with other indices of social competence, such as popularity (i.e., how well-liked one is by the peer group). Behaviors such as friendliness, smiling, cooperating, respecting peer norms, and clear communication were identified using this approach. Advantages to this approach include simplicity of creating a list of target behaviors that create a good basis for assessment checklists and intervention programming. However, weaknesses have also been identified with this method. Using different methods to select relevant skills has led to disagreement on criteria. This approach also locates social competence within the individual rather than as a function of interactions with others. Finally, the focus on individual social skills may fail to capture a full understanding of an individual's social competence. It is possible that someone may possess these social skills in isolation yet be unable to integrate them to function effectively with their peers.

Using sociometric status, or how well-liked one is by their peer group, is a common measure of social skills. An important strength of this method is that it captures the combined judgments of peers and includes both behavioral and affective aspects of social competence. These assessments also demonstrate good temporal stability and are both concurrently (at the same time) and predicatively (over time) associated with other indices of adjustment. These assessments can be useful for identifying those who lack social competence, but since they do not reveal why an individual struggles socially, they are not useful for designing social skills intervention. Finally, sociometric assessments do not measure an individual's ability to initiate and maintain social relationships, which may require different skills and could perhaps be a better predictor of social competence.

The ability to form social relationships is important for typical development. In this approach, social competence is measured by the quality of an individual's social relationships, which depends on both individuals. Social relationships can be horizontal, such as those with peers, and vertical, such as those with a parent or teacher. In the horizontal relationship, the skills of both partners are reflected relatively equally, while in a vertical relationship, the skills of the more skilled partner are more heavily reflected. This can serve as scaffolding to help increase social skills for the less-skilled social partner. The quality of a friendship can also be a significant predictor of adjustment.

5. What serves as the basis for friendship? How do people become friends?

You may think back to being a young child and how easy it seemed to make friends. You both liked playing with dolls or trucks, you both enjoyed soccer or tennis, you both loved to play on the playground, and you became nearly instant friends. As you've gotten older, you may have noticed that it no longer seems as simple to make friends. If you have, you are not alone in this sentiment. There are several reasons why making friends may seem to become more challenging as you get older. First, we tend to meet fewer people the older we get. Especially once you are out of school, you tend to encounter less new people on a day-to-day basis. As you become an adult, your priorities also tend to change. When you are a child, fun can be one of your main priorities, but as we get older, we have to begin to focus on other priorities, such as work, making money, romantic relationships, and ultimately (potentially) our own children. As such, sometimes making friends takes a backseat to these other priorities. Also, making new friends can be intimidating! As we get older, we realize that if we ask someone to be our friend, there is a chance that we will be rejected and they will say they don't want to be our friend. Thus, we can become afraid of being rejected, and then we no longer put ourselves out there to meet new people who could potentially become our friends. For some, they may have been burned by friends in the past. If this is the case, given their past, they may avoid trying to make new friends to avoid toxic relationships and being taken advantage of by others. Although all of these things can make it more challenging to make friends as you become an adult, building and maintaining friendships as an adult remains important and worthwhile. Research has shown that investing in close relationships is associated with better physical health, happiness, and socioemotional well-being in adulthood. Moreover, research has shown that making friends as an adult can be hard and takes time. One study found that two people need to spend 90 hours together to become friends or 200 hours to become close friends!

Some have discussed treating making friends like one treats dating. With this approach, the first step is courtship. Think about the type of friend you would like to meet. What is it that you are looking for? Try to answer the following questions for yourself: What kind of person do I love to spend time with? What made my friendship(s) from childhood so special? What type of person fits well with my personality? What kind of activities would I love to do with a friend? Once you answer these questions, you'll have an idea of what you are looking for in a friend. Next, think about where you might meet someone with these qualities (e.g., places, clubs, classes, groups). Also, do your best to become comfortable striking up and maintaining conversation with strangers. Friendships start by talking. You can comment on the weather, something you were watching on TV last night, or anything to make light conversation. Any kind of small talk will do. The important thing is that you are talking.

The next step we encounter in dating (for friends or romantic relationships) is flirting. One of the biggest mistakes we can make is never asking someone to hang out with us because we worry about being rejected by them. Another mistake we can make is going too fast. If you move too fast into a friendship, you might find that this is not the kind of person that you want to be friends with after all. When you "flirt," this can help you to avoid these mistakes. You can do this by seeing if you enjoy the same things. You can talk about the concert that you went to last week, your favorite sports team, where they are from, a new book you've been wanting to read, or you can ask them what they are going to do this weekend.

This way you can test the waters to see what you have in common and see if you connect with one another. It may also be important that your friends have similar values as you. This is important since our friends are a key source of emotional support for us. As you get to know someone, you'll get a sense of whether your values align with one another's. One way you can get a sense of this is to divulge something to your friend. Share something little with them to help begin to build trust. Finally, try to get a sense of how this person makes you feel. Do you enjoy the time you spend together? Do they make you laugh? Are you intrigued the more you talk to them? You want to find friends who make you feel good when you are around them and when you think about them.

The next step is pursuing the friend(s) whom you are interested in getting to know further. Think about the favorite things that you enjoy. If you have a favorite Chinese restaurant and your potential friend says that they love Chinese food too, this is a perfect opportunity to suggest that you get together for dinner there. Alternatively, maybe there is something new you've really been wanting to try. Perhaps you've really been wanting to try yoga or to join a dodgeball team. You can throw this idea out there to your new potential friend, as it's always nice to try something new with a partner in crime. Another way to connect with someone new is to offer to lend something to them. Maybe you have a favorite book or favorite article of clothing that you could offer to lend to them. Maybe you are learning to cook, and you could invite your new friend over to try some of the food you're learning to cook. Maybe your friend is getting ready to graduate from college and apply for jobs, and you're an English major. You could offer to edit their résumé for them. Finally, we all go through difficult times. If there is something that is bothering you, try bringing this up to your new friend. If they respond in a way that is supportive and you believe they are there for you, this is a good indication that you've got a friend on your hands. Look to see if they follow up with you to see how you are doing, too.

Finally, just like any romantic relationship, you want to determine if your friend has staying power. Is this someone whom you will want to have as a close friend over time? How do you decide this? In addition to continuing to get to know them, there are a few questions you can ask yourself that will be helpful in this decision-making process. Do they seem to be genuinely happy for you when something good happens to you? Conversely, do you truly want what is best for them, even if it's not easy for you? And could you be stuck with this person for days? Once you find this close friend, be sure to work to maintain this friendship. Do your best to care about the things that are important to your friend. Check in with them when you know they are having a busy or difficult week. Learn what your friend cares about in life, what's important to them, and learn about their goals. Then, support your friend in trying to achieve those goals. Lastly, don't avoid, and be able to have those difficult conversations with your friend. Friends challenge one another, call each other out when they are wrong, and sometimes have to deliver difficult news. When you do this, be gentle with your friend and treat them the way that you would want to be treated.

Psychologists have other recommendations for those who would like to make friends. First, it is important to like and feel comfortable with yourself in order to help yourself build healthy friendships. Thinking about what you like about yourself can help draw others to you. You can also find something that you feel passionate about. Take that first yoga class, take a class to learn sign language, go to the climbing gym, or volunteer for a cause you care about. These are all places where you can find friendships. As hard as it can be, putting yourself out there is the key to making new friends. Once you meet someone whom you'd like to get to know better, you should initially meet in a neutral public place. This can lessen some of the pressures you might have compared to inviting them to your home or dorm. When you meet this person, be a good listener and ask questions about your new companion. It is amazing how hard it can be to find someone who is a good listener, and this will not go unnoticed by your new companion. Finally, try not to expect too much from your new friend. No one person can provide you with everything you need, so it is important to go into a new relationship with realistic expectations and to try to have a variety of friends for different reasons.

There are a few final things to keep in mind when trying to make new friends. Assume the best in others and that they want to make new friends too. It is inherently awkward and uncomfortable to make new friends, but everyone is in the same position at some point in time. However, being vulnerable is the first step that opens you up to making a new friend. Remember too that people will like you more than you think they will. We tend to be our own worst critics. Chances are that you will actually brighten other peoples' days when you take that first step and reach out to them. Remember that it is OK to prioritize making and keeping friends. Having friends can be one of the most rewarding parts of life, so investing time and energy in friendship is necessary and worthwhile.

6. What contributes to high-quality friendship?

Children, adolescents, and adults all agree on the types of prosocial behaviors that are expected from our friends. Specifically, friends should help one another, share with one another, praise one another's successes, and encourage each other after they fail. However, there are some features of friendship that are recognized as important by adolescents but not by children. Self-disclosure of personal thoughts and feelings—"Best friends tell each other everything"—is valued during adolescence. In addition, adolescents say that friends stick up for one another in a fight to demonstrate their loyalty. Researchers have also described characteristics of good friendship, including prosocial behavior, self-esteem support, intimacy, and loyalty. Importantly, research has found that when individuals rate their friendship as high in a positive feature (such as intimacy), they tend to rate all positive features highly. This suggests that all of the positive features of friendship are linked to a single dimension of friendship quality.

Although positive features are indicative of friendship quality, even best friendships have negative qualities as well. Children and adolescents admit that they have conflict with their friends, but indicate that they still think of one another as equals. Friends report the co-occurrence of conflicts, dominance attempts ("My friends try to prove they're better than me"), and rivalry. These negative dimensions of friendship quality are only weakly correlated with the positive aspects of friendship quality.

Importantly, having high-quality friendships can have a positive impact on adolescent's and young adult's well-being. Specifically, high-quality friendship is associated with fostering self-esteem, improving social adjustment, and increasing the ability to cope with stressors. Among early adolescents in particular, having friendships with more positive features correlates with greater involvement in school, higher self-perceived social acceptance, and higher self-esteem. Furthermore, high-quality friendships tend to be more stable and long-lasting than low-quality friendships, and they are more likely to contribute to positive psychological adjustment. In addition, high-quality friendships are more apt to serve as emotional and cognitive resources that can help one adapt to stress and provide a sense of security and protection. If an adolescent or young adult lacks a high-quality friendship, he or she is more susceptible to a lack of social support. High-quality friendships also provide a positive model for what future relationships should look like, such as providing experience with intimacy, collaboration, and mutual negotiation. Experience with high-quality relationships also helps one to develop prosocial skills and competencies that are valuable in future relationships.

So, why is it that some adolescents and young adults have a relatively easy time establishing high-quality friendships, while others struggle to establish friendships or have friendships with low levels of support and intimacy and high levels of conflict and rivalry? Importantly, it appears that one's earliest relationships with parents/primary caregivers set the stage for high-quality friendship. Specifically, secure parent-child/caregiver attachment is strongly associated with children's ability to establish high-quality friendships. Additionally, authoritative (warm and supportive yet demanding) parenting is associated with peer competence and high levels of intimacy in adolescent friendship. Specific parenting practices also contribute to children's high-quality friendships. Adolescents who have parents who were more involved in consulting and helping them mediate peer relationships reported higher levels of positive friendship features. Similarly, higher autonomy provided to adolescents was associated with lower levels of conflict in friendships, and higher levels of parental monitoring have also been associated with lower levels of conflict. For girls, higher levels of parental monitoring are also related to positive friendship features (disclosure, help, and support).

Although children and adolescents are not directly involved in their parents' marital relationship, it may still have an important impact on their friendships and quality of those friendships. It is likely that marital quality impacts an adolescent's friendship quality via their parent-child attachment relationship. From a social learning perspective, the parental relationship serves as a model for children's friendships. Children learn important social skills (e.g., conflict negotiation, communication skills) through direct instruction and observation of their parents. Finally, from a family system's perspective, the family context and familial relationships would be expected to influence a child and adolescent's adjustment and their social relationships. Several studies have lent support to the idea that parents' marital quality impacts children's and adolescent's friendship quality. Marital quality has predicted children's friendship quality, and poor parental conflict resolution has been associated with lower-quality friendships with poor conflict resolution and low levels of intimacy and companionship. In addition, parents' own friendship participation may impact their children's and adolescent's friendship quality. When mothers rated their own friendships as supportive, their children and adolescents reported higher levels of intimacy and closeness in their best friendships.

It is plausible that children and adolescents' relationships with their siblings may also have an impact on their friendship quality; however, research findings have been mixed in this area. One study found no difference in the number or quality of friendships as a function or whether or not a child had siblings. In another study, children rated by their mothers as having very positive friendships were found to be competitive and controlling in their sibling relationships. It is possible that children and adolescents can dedicate their energy only adequately to friendship or sibling relationships or that high-quality friendship might compensate for difficult sibling relations.

The most-studied feature that contributes to friendship quality is gender. Hormonal differences between boys and girls are believed to contribute to different play styles. Girls tend to have a calmer play style, while boys tend to have a rougher play style. As a result, children are drawn to same-sex playmates. It appears that due to the different nature of friendship, there are structural differences in how friendship qualities are defined for the genders. For instance, companionship has been found to be a stronger component of intimacy for adolescent boys than girls. Girls reported higher levels of intimacy, and boys reported higher levels of peer control. Similarly, emotional closeness for boys was determined by shared experience and self-disclosure, while self-disclosure alone was predictive for girls. As such, the friendships of boys and girls tend to differ in important ways.

One final important contributor to friendship quality is peer rejection. Despite the fact that low-accepted children are not well-liked by the peer group, many of these children are able to establish close friendships. However, it may be expected that these friendships are lower in quality given the social skills and social information processing deficits of rejected children and adolescents. The friends of rejected children do tend to be younger, less accepted by their peers, and more likely to originate outside of school as compared to friends of high-accepted children. These friendships also tend to be less stable than the relationships of high-accepted children. When these friends are observed during play, they are noted to show less positive social behavior, less coordinated play, and less sensitivity with one another and to have more disagreements. Girls who are rejected by their peers demonstrated poorer and more immature conflict resolution skills than their better accepted peers. However, observers rated the quality of these friendships similarly. When children and adolescents report on their own friendship quality, sometimes differences are found where lower-accepted children rate their friendships as lower in quality, whereas other studies find no differences in friendship quality.

Different and Changing Friendships

7. How stable is friendship?

Given that friendship is a voluntary social relationship (unlike familial relations), it is often assumed that friendship is more likely to end than family relationships. However, since friendship plays a distinct role in development (e.g., promoting social skills, social support), it seems plausible that friendships must be enduring in order to provide the companionship, intimacy, and closeness that are the major benefits of having friends. Importantly, it appears that friendship stability increases with age. By middle childhood (fourth grade), 75 percent of friendships are maintained over the course of a school year. However, instability is also noted among friendship groups as only about 30 percent of friendship cliques remain stable over a year. Early adolescence appears to be a period of particular instability in friendships. One-third to one-half of friendships are unstable during this developmental period, when youth are regularly losing old friendships and forming new ones. This may be because this coincides with the transition to high school and the significant social, biological, and cognitive changes that accompany puberty. Once youth pass through the turmoil of early adolescence, friendship stability appears to increase. Research has found that adolescents retain between 50 and 75 percent of friendships over the course of a school year. In addition, adolescents tend to lose more old friends than gain new ones, and the number of close friendships decreases significantly during this developmental period.

This may reflect the importance of increased intimacy during this time, such that fewer but closer relationships are desired. Moderate to high stability in adolescent social networks has been found with 50–80 percent of cliques remaining intact over a year.

There are several factors that have been proposed to account for friendship stability, including relational and contextual factors. The majority of research has been conducted on same-sex friendships, but cross-sex friendships become increasingly prevalent and important during adolescence. Initially, these friendships tend to be short-lived and less stable than same-sex friendships. This increase in cross-sex friendships is more pronounced for girls than boys, and girls report greater cross-sex friendship instability than do boys. This may be because girls' cross-sex friendships tend to be with older boys from outside their school. Friendship stability may also vary based on friends' similarity with regard to race and ethnicity. Studies generally have found that cross-race friendships are less stable than same-race friendships. However, cross-race friendships do not differ significantly from same-race friendships in terms of friendship provisions with the exception of intimacy. Cross-race friendships are viewed as less intimate than same-race friendships. Cross-race friendships are noted to decline over time, particularly after the transition to high school.

Additionally, there are several features of friendship that affect the friendship's stability. Research clearly demonstrates that friendship quality predicts friendship stability. A number of studies have found a positive link between high-quality friendship and friendship stability. Similarly, negative aspects of friendship have also been noted to impact friendship stability. High levels of conflict within the friendship have been linked to lower friendship stability. In particular, the type of conflict resolution skills used in a friendship may be important—confrontational and assertive strategies in response to friendship conflict have been found to help girls maintain friendship, while the tendency to minimize problems has been positively associated with friendship stability for boys. Probably not surprisingly, when adolescents change schools (such as transition to high school, attend a new school due to relocation), friendship stability decreases. In addition, youth who move to new communities are noted to have lower levels of intimacy and companionship in their friendships. When looking at gender, it is not fully clear whether girls or boys have greater stability in their friendships. Several studies have not found gender differences in friendship stability during childhood. Studies that have found gender differences in friendship stability lean toward boys having slightly more stable friendships than girls.

Since children and adolescents differ in behavioral characteristics, these have been examined to determine whether they relate to friendship stability. Research has revealed that individuals who are depressed maintain a negatively biased view of their own friendships such that they perceive themselves as having lower friendship quality with their best friends and as having lower levels of peer acceptance. In addition, increased levels of depressive symptoms significantly predict increased friendship instability one month later. In contrast, although shyness/withdrawal is associated with lower-quality friendships, shy/withdrawn youth are just as likely as nonwithdrawn children to have stable best friendships over the course of a school year. It is plausible that as shyness becomes more salient to peers with age, this may lead to greater difficulty in maintaining friendships. The experience of peer victimization may also be linked to friendship instability. Children and adolescents who experience victimization tend to experience difficulty forming new friendships. For girls, if both girls are victimized, the friendship remains relatively stable, but when only one girl is victimized, the friendship is more likely to end. Those who maintain stable friendships are reported to display low levels of peer victimization. In contrast, those who lost friendships became more victimized over time, whereas those who gained friendships over time became less victimized. Youth who experience externalizing difficulties tend to have lower friendship stability. Girls who have attention deficit hyperactivity disorder have been found to have difficulty making and maintaining friendships. They were more likely to have no friends and less likely to have multiple friends. In addition, their friendships were characterized by more negative friendship features (e.g., conflict, relational aggression). Another research study found that both relational and overt aggression predicts friendship instability. Antisocial adolescents tend to have lower-quality friendships, and their friendships are more conflictual, are shorter in duration, and end inappropriately. Finally, friendship instability has also been found to predict an increase in antisocial behavior over time.

8. How does friendship change during adolescence?

Adolescence (13–19 years old) involves significant changes in physical and cognitive development, and it is accompanied by major changes in social relationships. Adolescence is a crucial period for social development as close friendship becomes increasingly important to socioemotional adjustment, teens expand their social networks, and romantic relationships emerge. Teens experience several important transitions during adolescence, including the challenging transitions to middle school and high school. As part of these milestones, teens' network of peers increases, and those whom they associate with within the peer crowd becomes an important aspect of their peer relationships. Notably, adolescence marks the time when close friends surpass parents/caregivers as the primary source of social support. At the onset of puberty, there tends to be a desire for increased autonomy and emotional distance from parents/caregivers and a shift to a more intense focus on friendship and social interaction. This is a normal transition where increased focus on peers marks a healthy and important new stage in development. However, less contact with one's family does not mean that family closeness is unimportant. In fact, studies have confirmed that attachment and close relationships with family and parental/caregiver monitoring remain the most important factors associated with not engaging in risk behaviors (i.e., not smoking, less use of alcohol and other drugs, later initiation of sexual intercourse, and fewer suicide attempts) among adolescents.

There are several developmental changes that occur in peer relationships during the adolescent period. In particular, teens spend more time with friends and often report feeling understood and accepted in these relationships. Less time is typically spent with family during the adolescent period than during the childhood years. Adolescents tend to select their friends based on similar attitudes, values, and shared activities. In contrast, common activities, alone, tend to be the basis for the formation of friendships during childhood. Teens who are friends with one another also tend to have similar educational interests and similar involvement in school. Friends help teens refine their social skills, offer a context for trying out new activities and ideas, and provide social support and encouragement. Friendship provides a context for teens to learn about themselves, who they want to be, and what they want to do in life. When adolescents identify with their peers, this helps shape their values and moral judgments and define how they differ and how they may be similar to their parents. Peers expose adolescents to the world outside their family, and the peer groups with whom adolescents associate provide a source of acceptance, popularity, status, and prestige.

A cornerstone of peer relationships during adolescence is close, dyadic (one-to-one), reciprocal (where both individuals view one another as friends) friendship. During this developmental period, friendship begins to make more significant contributions to well-being and socioemotional adjustment than peer acceptance (how well one is liked by their peer group). Specifically, friendship during adolescence serves important functions for both self-esteem and social-emotional adjustment. Adolescent friendship is characterized by higher levels of intimacy, loyalty, and self-disclosure than childhood friendship. This close sharing helps teens to explore their own identity and sense of self. The intimacy and trust unique to adolescent friendships provide opportunities to experiment with different identities. Although this closeness is not unique to female friendships, it appears to serve a particularly important function for girls' and young women's well-being. Females tend to value the feeling that they can freely share their private thoughts and feelings as a key feature of friendship. In contrast, the friendships of adolescent boys and young men tend to be based more around common activities and validation of worth through actions than intimacy. Boys and men tend to engage in more action-oriented pursuits, while girls and women spend more time talking with one another. All adolescents, however, tend to value the same qualities in a friend: loyalty, trustworthiness, and frankness.

Of critical importance to adolescent adjustment is having at least one reciprocal close friendship that can contribute to resilience. Adolescents who have at least one close friend have been found to have higher feelings of self-worth at age 30 when compared to teens who were friendless. Additionally, mutual friendship during adolescence is linked to better self-image and better school performance. The number of friends that teens have tends to vary, and adolescents who are introverted often report having fewer close friendships, but just one friend appears to be the magic number. Having just one friend can serve as a psychological buffer. As such, building a close, reciprocated friendship appears to be a critical developmental task of adolescence.

Peer group involvement and friendship tend to change over the course of adolescence. In early adolescence, students tend to have one primary same-sex peer group with whom they identify. Acceptance by the peer group is of great importance to early adolescents, and conformity tends to be at its peak. However, by the middle of adolescence (14–16 years), peer groups tend to be mixed sex (boys and girls together), and conformity decreases as the peer group becomes more tolerant of individual differences in appearance, feelings, and beliefs. By late adolescence, there is even less focus on acceptance by the overall peer group, which is replaced by the critical importance of close dyadic friendships and ultimately romantic relationships, with the majority of adolescents reporting having had a dating relationship by the time they were 16 years old.

9. How does friendship change during adulthood?

The cornerstones of friendship during adolescence and young adulthood are self-disclosure and social support. During intimate conversation, friends share secrets, feelings, and problems and provide one another with emotional support and validation. Friends tend to be the most likely confidants that young adults turn to when they are in distress. The seminal work of Harry Stack Sullivan (1953) revealed why adolescence and early adulthood is a critical period for intimate friendship. This period represents a time in development when individuals are motivated to develop relationships outside the family to fulfill their intimacy needs. As friends begin to disclose more to one another, they in turn provide social support to their friend. More recent theories emphasize the transitions that occur in social networks with the entrance to adulthood, including relationships with parents, romantic partners, and one's own children. Specifically, Carberry and Burhrmester (1998) emphasized three major transitional phases: the single uncommitted phase, the married without children phase, and the married with young children phase. A young adult's time, emotional investment, and the functional significance of friendship is believed to vary based on these other relational roles. Different family role commitments likely impact the amount of time and emotional energy available to invest in friendships, and thus influence intimacy in friendships. Additionally, when one takes on a new role (e.g., spouse, parent), this may create new sources of social support, reducing the intimacy needs of friendships. Similar theories propose that as individuals take on significant involvement in romantic relationships, less emotional investment will be put toward friendships.

The research evidence on late adolescence and young adulthood appears to be mixed. For instance, some studies during late adolescence and young adulthood indicate increased self-disclosure, more social support, and more intimacy than in earlier friendships. However, other studies suggest that intimacy, commitment, and satisfaction decrease during the transition to late adolescence. It is possible that this coincides with the emergence of new social roles (e.g., romantic partners) that are more prominent. Modern studies that have examined friendships and romantic relationships simultaneously have found that romantic partners become the major source of intimacy. Adolescents and young adults who have romantic partners spend significantly less time with family and friends than similar young adults who do not have a romantic partner. During young adulthood, the proportion of individuals who choose romantic partners as their closest friends doubles, whereas that of those who choose nonromantic friends significantly declines. Moreover, the intimacy of romantic relationships is rated as higher than the intimacy of friendships. Intimacy, social support, and attachment are more commonly reported features of romantic relationships than friendships during this developmental period.

Although the research previously mentioned might suggest that romantic involvement decreases friendship quality, some studies in fact suggest that it may have little impact on friendship quality. Specifically, research has found that late adolescents do not differ in the amount of social support received from a best friend whether or not they had a romantic partner, and married and single adults do not differ in their perceptions of friendship intimacy. However, research suggests that as young adults become more involved and committed in their romantic relationships, their friendships may become less intimate as their romantic relationship begins to take the place of friendship involvement. Finally, research findings suggest that as an individual begins to have children, friendships decrease in number and importance. For example, from pregnancy to the postpartum period, women report a decrease in the number of friends and an increase in the number of family members in their primary social support network. They also rate their instrumental and emotional support from friends lower than that from their family members.

Although friendship continues to develop during adulthood, relatively fewer researchers have focused on this aspect of adult friendship. In particular, friendships during mid-life are understudied. Older adults tend to be less likely to define friendship according to frequent, face-to-face contact, but they are more likely to maintain friendship through letters and phone calls. As adults age, there are several constraints placed upon the maintenance and development of friendships. Widowhood, relocation, and the social context of very late life tend to exert a negative influence on friendship maintenance. Moreover, with increased disability that comes with age, the basic reciprocity of friendship can be challenged.

10. In what ways are the friendships of boys/girls and men/women the same, and how are they different?

Researchers have explored the similarities and differences between boys' and girls' and men's and women's friendships. Overall, there tend to be more similarities than differences between the genders, but there are some important differences that have been found. The most prominent finding is that female friendships tend to be more intimate (i.e., the sharing of feelings, providing emotional support) and supportive, while male friendships tend to be more "instrumental" and "transactional." Boys' and men's friendships tend to be based on common or shared activities, such as sporting events, music, or video games. Boys and men may also be more likely to reciprocate favors and work on projects together with friends than are girls and women. When social class is taken into account, working-class men tend to have reciprocity with material goods (e.g., exchanging tools or books), while middle-class men are more likely to report sharing leisure activities (e.g., attending sporting events) with their friends. It appears that girls and women generally are more invested in their friendships than boys and men as evidenced by their efforts to maintain the relationship, such as meeting up with friends more often, calling friends, and making efforts to keep in touch. It may be that boys and men do not feel as compelled to stay as connected to their friends. Although male friendships tend to be less intimate and supportive than female friendships, there is some evidence that indicates that female friendships tend to be more fragile than male friendships.

During adolescence, there tend to be gender differences in friendship quality. When you ask teens to describe their friendships, girls will often say that they get together to "just talk," and their interactions tend to contain more self-disclosure and supportive statements. As such, girls' friendships appear to be more emotionally close than those of boys. Boys tend to discuss accomplishments, and their friendships involve more competition and conflict than girls' friendships, and they are more likely to gather together for an activity than to just talk. However, this does not mean that boys do not form close friendships. It just seems that their friendship quality is more variable than girls' friendship quality. When ethnically diverse boys from low-income families were asked to describe their friendships, African American, Asian American, and Hispanic males mentioned that their friendships were characterized by closeness, mutual support, and self-disclosure more often than their white counterparts did. However, as these ethnic minority boys transitioned from mid- to late-adolescence many reported a decline in friendship closeness. It is possible that the masculine stereotypes to be tough and unemotional may have interfered with their friendship bonds. Hispanic boys were less likely to conform to this gender stereotype, perhaps due to the cultural value of emotional expressiveness between male friends. This allowed these boys to benefit from the supportiveness of intimate friendship that is consistently related to better emotional adjustment.

Importantly, the closeness that girls and women have in their friendships can come at a cost. When friends focus on deep feelings and thoughts, they tend to "co-ruminate." This means that you repeatedly mull over problems and negative emotions, and girls are more likely to engage in this behavior than are boys. Importantly, co-rumination can bring friends together by contributing to higher friendship quality, but it can also trigger symptoms of anxiety and depression. When teenagers are depressed, they are more likely to redirect these co-ruminative conversations to focus on their own problems, which increases the likelihood that they will be rejected by their friends. When conflict arises in these more intimate friendships, the potential exists for one friend to harm the other through relational aggression, for instance, by divulging sensitive personal information to others. This is one factor that contributes to girls' friendships, on average, being of shorter duration than boys' friendships.

As children get older, these and other gender differences in what they expect to get from friendship emerge. Girls and women are more likely than boys and men to desire closeness and dependency in friendships and also worry about abandonment, loneliness, hurting others, peers' evaluations, and loss of relationships if they were to express anger. By age 12, girls view their friendships as more intimate than boys do, and they view their friendships as providing more validation, care, help, and guidance. Girls are also more likely to report friendship-related stress, such as when a friend breaks off a friendship or reveals their problems to other friends, and greater stress from dealing emotionally with stressors their friends experience.

However, there are also several ways in which girls' and boys' and women's and men's friendships are similar. Specifically, both genders report similar amounts of conflict in their best friendships. Their friendships also do not differ much in terms of the recreational opportunities they provide (e.g., doing this together, going to one another's houses), although the activities that each gender participates in do tend to differ (e.g., shopping versus sports).

11. What are cross-gender friendships like, and when do they typically form?

If you think back to your friendships from childhood, you will likely realize that all or nearly all of those friends were of the same sex/gender. Prior to adolescence, very little social interaction occurs between boys and girls. This gender segregation is voluntary, and other-sex friendships are relatively uncommon during childhood. The fact that girls and boys typically do not associate with one another leads to very different peer experiences during childhood. However, around early adolescence other-sex contact begins to increase significantly. Nine-year-olds, on average, have less than one other-sex friend, while thirteen-year-olds have an average of more than five other-sex friends. Other researchers have reported that the number of other-sex friends increases substantially between sixth and eighth grade. Same-sex friendships continue to be important to adolescents, but other-sex friendships gain importance as adolescence progresses. Similar to the move away from reliance on parent-child relationships during adolescence, the move toward other-sex friendships is also a significant social transformation during this developmental period. The transition to other-sex relationships happens gradually. Even when early adolescents show a preference for other-sex friendships over same-sex friendships, they continue to be more involved in same-sex friendships than other-sex friendships. Early research in this area did not distinguish between other-sex friendships and heterosexual romantic relationships. However, this may be an important distinction to make as adolescents do discriminate between other-sex friendships and romantic relationships. Teens characterize their other-sex friendships by affiliation, while they characterize their romantic relationships by affiliation, intimacy, and passion. Mixed-sex interactions that become normative during early adolescence tend to precede dating and romantic relationships, which are less common during this developmental period. It does seem that other-sex friendships and romantic relationships are linked to one another. Adolescents who have a larger number of other-sex friends are more likely to develop romantic relationships. Other-sex friendships not only provide some of the same benefits as same-sex friendships but also offer additional benefits, such as perspective on the other sex, which adolescents may not have been privy to previously. In addition to fostering romantic relationships, other-sex friendships also seem to influence the nature of these relationships. Having more contact with other-sex friends has been found to contribute to longer romantic relationships, and those romantic relationships are described as being based on self-disclosure rather than social status.

So, it is clear that other-sex friendships tend to emerge during adolescence, but what functions do these relationships serve? Do they simply serve similar functions to same-sex friendships, or is there something new and different that these relationships provide during adolescence and early adulthood? Affiliation appears to be a key role of both same-sex and other-sex friendships. This descriptor also seems to be a key in romantic relationships. Other-sex friend networks provide opportunities for adolescents to develop these affiliative skills with other-sex peers. These skills are expected to help facilitate intimacy and support when they develop romantic relationships. At the same time, the sexual system is playing a central role. For heterosexual youth, the interest in the opposite sex increases around puberty, and teens are faced with the challenges of coping with sexual feelings and learning to act on these feelings appropriately. Gay and lesbian youth are presented with the additional challenge of deciding whether or not they are attracted to other-sex peers or same-sex peers and grappling with these feelings.

The relationships that adolescents develop with other-sex peers during adolescence lay the groundwork for adult other-sex inter-actions. Generally, having an other-sex friend is associated with posi-tive self-perceptions. Gender may play a differing role here. Boys may express an interest in having a girlfriend during early adolescence, but the actual dating experience may lead to a decline in confidence while figuring out this new social role. For girls, research has found that early sexual involvement is associated with deviancy and poor psychosocial adjustment.

Other-sex friendships provide unique opportunities for both healthy development and unfavorable development. These relationships are important for healthy development because they offer opportunities to develop the interpersonal skills needed for success in mixed-sex social and work environments that are encountered during young adulthood and throughout the rest of life. Other-sex relationships also provide learning opportunities to interact productively with individuals who have different experiences, interests, and backgrounds. Unfortunately, having a greater proportion of other-sex friends during adolescence has been associated with experiencing some form of potentially offensive sexual behaviors.

12. Why does friendship often change when a friend forms a new romantic relationship?

Nearly everyone has had the experience where a good friend of theirs starts dating someone new and seems to drop off the face of the earth. They are no longer hanging out with you all the time, calling you, or maybe not even texting you to see how you are doing and to update you on their life. To some extent, this is understandable as you know they are focused on the new relationship, but it can still hurt and negatively impact your friendship when it happens.

Recent research shows that being in a romantic relationship really does change you. In particular, adolescents tend to become more like their dating partners and less like their friends once they enter a romantic relationship. In one study, researchers asked 12- to 19-year-old boys and girls questions about their friends, romantic partners, and alcohol use and abuse. They found that friends who were in relationships had less similar attitudes toward alcohol abuse than did their single friends. The similarity between the friends' attitudes toward alcohol abuse dropped when one or both friends started dating, and their attitudes toward alcohol abuse became more similar to their romantic partner. This did not, however, translate into a higher risk for substance abuse but just that the source of influence changed. The researchers concluded that this lends support to the idea that romantic partners do in fact serve as a distraction from friendships.

If being in a new romantic relationship does change you, in what ways might this happen? First, it is possible that you may not be able to completely relate to your single friends anymore. For instance, you may no longer commiserate with your friends over bad first dates, dating apps, and relationship woes when you are happy in your relationship. It is also possible that your being in a relationship may create some self-doubt in your friends, particularly when your friends are putting pressure on themselves to be in romantic relationships or to get married. When you form a new romantic relationship, it is also possible that this will help you to form new friendships. As you meet new people and form new friendships, it is natural for your other friendships to change and evolve. Unfortunately, a new relationship can sometimes contribute to the end of a friendship. If your friend is unable to accept your new relationship (despite your best efforts to continue to include them in your life), it might mean that it is time to end the friendship. Conversely, it is also possible that being in a new relationship could actually bring you closer to your friend. You may bond with your friend over his or her past relationships, now that you are in a similar position. Your new significant other may also be able to introduce your friend to new potential love interests.

So, what can you do if you have recently started dating someone but it is important to you to maintain strong friendships? First, be sure to take time out of your busy schedule to see one another. If you really care about your friend, you'll make the effort to see them in person. Texting and social media are great for keeping in touch, but they are no match for face-to-face interaction. You should not only get together on your own with your friend but also include him or her in things you do in groups with your significant other so that they feel included and can get to know the new important person in your life. When you do get together with your friend, really be there. Make sure that you aren't checking your phone and be mindful of having equality in your conversation. Make sure that you listen as much as you speak. You can also let your new romantic partner know how important your friends are to you and that you plan to keep your friends as a priority in your life. If your friend is also dating someone, try planning a double or group date. This can be a great opportunity to see how your friends and your significant other mesh, and getting together in a group can take off some of the pressure of individual interactions. Next, make sure that you continue to be there for your friend. If they are going through something challenging, make sure to be there to listen and lend a shoulder to cry on, if needed. In return, your friend will continue to be there for you when you need to vent about your significant other or other stressors in your life. Even though you are likely now even busier adding a significant other to your life, be sure to continue to check in on your friends. Send them a quick text just to let them know that you are thinking of them and that you want to see how they are doing or meet up for coffee or tea to chat. Remember when you get into a relationship you are still "you." Try your best not to lose sight of yourself in the relationship, and remember what made you "you" before you became part of the romantic relationship. Finally, keep in mind that you are friends because you want to be. Just like you have to invest time and energy into your romantic relationship to sustain it, the same goes for your friendships as well.

Alternatively, if your friend has recently entered a relationship and you are single and feel your friend slipping away, there are some things that you can do for your friendship and for yourself as well. You can try giving your friendship a little time and space. It may just be that your friend and your relationship need a little time to adjust to the change. However, you definitely don't just have to wait it out and hope that things get better. You can also talk directly to your friend about your concerns and try to work out a way to keep your relationship going strong. When you talk, you can set up expectations for your friendship. If you tell your friend what you need and they talk about their expectations in return, you may feel happier moving forward. For instance, you could tell your friend how much you love getting together to watch your favorite TV show or the football game each week and see if this is something that can be maintained. Do your best to stay positive. Adjusting to change can be hard, but things do tend to settle down over time. If, however, your friendship is really bringing you down, it may be time to take a break from the relationship. You could work to distract yourself by focusing on your interests or a new hobby. Sometimes expressing how you feel in other ways can also be helpful. You could write about how you are feeling in a journal, create art, dance, or sing, whatever appeals to you the most. If you find that your friendship has really changed and you do not see it getting better, it may be time to seek out new friends. If your feelings are really impacted by the loss of this relationship, it is OK to reach out to others for support. You could talk to other friends or family or reach out to a therapist or psychologist to discuss this difficult transition in your life. You don't have to go through it alone.

13. Can you be friends with people who are different from you?

The short answer to this question is yes, of course, you can be friends with someone who is different from you. However, the long answer is that it is not quite that simple. It is human nature to seek out and associate with people who are similar to you in any number of ways—religiously, politically, racially, and so on. This is called "sorting," and it can impact your friend network. The United States of America continues to become more racially and ethnically diverse. However, recent surveys find that relatively few adults say they have a lot in common with others who do not share their same racial background. This is particularly true for adults who are of only one race themselves. Among individuals who are single-race white, 62 percent say they have a lot in common with people in the United States who are white, while 1 in 10 or fewer say they have a lot in common with people who are black, Asian, or American Indian. A similar pattern of results is also found for adults who are single-race black or Asian. However, the majority of Americans report that they have at least some close friends who are white, black, Hispanic, or of mixed race. A somewhat smaller percentage say that they have close friends who are of Asian and American Indian origin. Adults who are multiracial are more likely than the general public to have at least some close friends of mixed race, black, or American Indian origin. Sixteen percent of multiracial adults say all or most of their close friends are multiracial, compared with only 6 percent of the general population. Although it is clear that friendship can transcend race and ethnicity, the two tend to be strongly correlated with one another. Individuals tend to have more friends among their own race than they do among races that are different than their own. Among adults who identify as fully white, 81 percent say that all or most of their close friends are also white. Among single-race blacks, 70 percent say that all or most of their close friends are black, and among fully Asian Americans, 54 percent say all or most of their close friends are Asian. For multiracial adults, their close friends tend to reflect their own mixed racial composition to some extent.

As one gets older, the likelihood of cross-race friendship becomes less likely. As such, it is important to foster conditions that encourage cross-race friendships during childhood and adolescence. This is important because cross-race friendships can provide many positive benefits. Research among adults has found that having more cross-race friends can promote more positive racial attitudes and also lower feelings of discomfort when interacting with someone of a different race. For children, cross-race friendships reduce feelings of vulnerability in the school context. They can also protect adolescents from the negative impacts of school-based discrimination, including feelings of loneliness and depressive symptoms, and can increase feelings of school belongingness. Research has demonstrated that there are at least five ways to increase the likelihood of intergroup friendships. First, if learning environments integrate children who are different from one another, this provides adolescents and young adults with more opportunities for intergroup contact and opportunities to make intergroup friendships. Second, it is important to teach children and adolescents the ability to differentiate between seeing differences and prejudice. This can be achieved by teaching empathy and perspective-taking and teaching about the social roots of prejudice. Third, exposing children and adolescents to models of intergroup friendships can be valuable. This can be as simple as exposing teens to books with cross-race friendships. Fourth, engage cross-groups of adolescents and young adults in cooperative tasks. Finally, it is important to encourage deep engagement among different social groups and build upon the understanding of our common humanity. When adolescents engage deeply with one another, this helps highlight our commonalities, rather than our differences, and in turn can encourage friendship formation.

Importantly, recent research among college students has found that friendships developed during the first year of college can endure and help bridge division and help embrace differences. The study surveyed over 7,000 first-year college students in 122 institutions that represented a range of different races and religions. Colleges can offer a unique opportunity where people of different beliefs have the ability to interact and get to know one another. For many students, this may be the first time they are exposed to others who are different from themselves in important ways. By the end of the first year of college, 64 percent of students who had no friendships with those who had a different worldview at the start of the year made at least one friend with a different worldview. Students of all faiths reported more inter-worldview friendships with people who were from different political backgrounds; were of a different sexual orientation; and were agnostic, atheist, Muslim, and Jewish. These students were appreciative of these worldviews even if they didn't share these worldviews themselves. Those young adults who developed friendships with those who had differing worldviews also generally developed positive attitudes toward others of all worldviews. These relationships also demonstrated resiliency with two-thirds maintaining these friendships despite worldview differences. In particular, 37 percent of students said they had a significant disagreement with a friend about religion but they remained friends, while 52 percent of students reported having a significant disagreement with a friend about politics and they remained friends.

There are several things that college campuses can do to help foster friendships among students who differ from one another. First, they can work to create a campus that is hospitable to students of various worldviews by providing spaces where students with different backgrounds and beliefs can interact. Second, campus-wide initiatives can be created to encourage students to reflect upon their friendships and understand the benefits of friendship across differences, and they can encourage contact and foster meaningful interactions among different groups.

The Impact of Friendship

14. What are the benefits of friendship?

Friendships begin forming early on in life. As early as preschool, children report having friends. Throughout our lives, friendships provide us with a host of positive benefits. One of the most important ways that friendship contributes to development is the context that it provides for social development. It offers a place to learn and practice different social skills and social competencies. The companionship, intimacy, and conflict that friendship provides contribute in important ways to the development of social competence.

It is no doubt that one of the key reasons we make friends is for companionship. Companionship involves spending time together, enjoying one another's company, and working together on activities. This aspect of friendship remains important across the full life span. Companionship involves sharing specific interests, spending time together across different settings, and talking with one another. The companionship provided by friends is different from that of just classmates. Friends know one another better, spend more time together, engage in more sophisticated activities, and have more in common with each other.

Intimacy is another key benefit of friendship. It may entail laughing with one another about inside jokes, sharing your worries and deepest secrets, and sharing hugs. The need for intimacy within friendship arises during preadolescence (between the ages of 9 and 12 years). During this time, same-gender friendships are a significant developmental accomplishment. Researchers have found that self-disclosure, a key component of intimacy, increases throughout adolescence. For girls, self-disclosure is the primary path to intimacy, while self-disclosure and shared activities lead to feelings of closeness for boys. Intimacy during adolescence has been linked to higher sociability, lower internalizing (anxiety/depression) distress, and higher self-esteem.

Conflict and the ways in which friends solve conflict are another important component of friendship. During adolescence, conflicts typically involve disagreements about interpersonal issues, and disagreements are often resolved by negotiation or disengagement from one another. You may wonder why I am talking about conflict as I discuss the benefits of friendship, but conflict can in fact be a benefit of friendship. Conflict offers friends opportunities to advance their communication skills, understand another person's perspective, and realize that others' behaviors and goals matter. Social perspective-taking is very important for resolving conflicts with friends.

Friends also play a key role in emotional development. Research suggests that during childhood and adolescence, individuals learn which emotions are socially and culturally acceptable to display to different interaction partners (i.e., friends, general peers, their mother, etc.). School-age children are more willing to express negative emotions to their parents than their friends, but they are more likely to express anger to their friends than to their mothers. It also appears that interactions with friends increase knowledge of emotions. In addition, improved emotional understanding influences interactions with friends in a positive manner. Similarly, the ability to regulate one's emotions also impacts friendship. Those who are better able to regulate their emotions tend to be better at both making and keeping friends. Friendship provides opportunities to negotiate conflict, cooperate, and promote connectedness, all of which contribute to the development of emotion regulation skills.

Interactions with friends also appear to contribute to cognitive development. Collaborating with friends can help to increase problem-solving skills, especially problem-solving skills for more difficult tasks. Friendship also provides a context to advance theory of mind skills. Theory of mind is the ability to understand the mental states (thoughts, beliefs, desires) of others and that these thoughts, beliefs, and desires can differ from your own. There is significantly less research linking friendship to cognitive development than there is social development, but it still appears to play an important role in this facet of development.

Most importantly, friendship can promote adaptive psychosocial adjustment. The emotional support that friends provide can help us to cope with life stress and transitions throughout life. Friends listen to us, offer a shoulder to lean on, give consistent and ongoing guidance, and provide us with a sense of being understood. By the time we become adolescents, the emotional support we receive from friends is the most important type of support that they can offer. Friends can offer important emotional support during times of school transition (i.e., transition to middle school, then to high school, and then to college). Moreover, friends can serve a protective emotional factor. It is possible that social support from friends may offer validation of our self-worth and thus enhance our ability to cope, or alternatively, positive experiences with friends may have the ability to compensate for negative social experiences in other realms (e.g., with parents, other peers). Even if one is not well-liked by their broader peer group, even having one close friendship can protect against feelings of anxiety and depression. Those who do not have friends tend to be lonelier, and loneliness tends to contribute to feelings of depression.

15. How can having a best friend during adolescence be good for you?

We have talked broadly about the important provisions that friendship can provide us, but there are also some specific benefits of having friends (and a best friend) during adolescence. Adolescence is a time when there are complex and dramatic changes taking place. During this time, adolescents' bodies are physically maturing, their self-awareness increases, they grow increasingly independent from their parents, and their social horizons expand as they develop intimate relationships and as they are exposed to more peers in differing contexts (larger schools, jobs, extracurricular activities). Advances in cognitive development allow for more abstract and logical thinking, and adolescents are faced with important questions that determine their futures. Friendship is so important during this developmental period because it contributes to many of these changes.

Research shows that most adolescents do have friends. Most will name one or two best friends and several other close friends. On average, adolescents spend three hours per day with their friends and receive an average of 80 text messages per day. Thus, it is clear that friends play an important role during this developmental period. During pre-adolescence, the need for interpersonal intimacy (closeness, empathy, love, and security) emerges. There also tends to be an increase in reciprocity (i.e., expectations of intimacy, common interests), commitment (i.e., loyalty, trust), and egalitarianism (i.e., shared power). Companionship continues to be valued, and friendship helps contribute to identity development. As one navigates through adolescence, the expectations from friends tend to increase, the number of conflicts and levels of exclusivity decrease, empathy and sharing increase, and attachment and intimacy remain stable or increase. During middle and later adolescence, other-sex friendships also emerge. It is not until college, however, that other-sex friends occupy as much time as same-sex friends. During adolescence, youth begin to spend less time with their parents and more time with their friends, and by age 16–18, emotional support from friends begins to exceed that of emotional support from parents. Friends also help adolescents make short-term decisions. Adjustment and well-being during adolescence seems to be dependent on support from both friends and parents.

Friends can play an important role in identity development during adolescence. This involves defining the self, determining life goals and direction, and identifying core values. Friends act as role models and provide an opportunity to "try on" different identities. Friends can play an important role in our own self-esteem, and their opinion of us impacts our self-concept. It appears that self-esteem is both an outcome of positive friendship experiences and a determinant of friendship experiences. This means that having a high-quality friendship may promote self-esteem and that adolescents with high self-esteem may be more capable of establishing positive friendships than adolescents with low self-esteem.

Another key task during adolescence is the emergence of romantic relationships. Friends contribute to the development of romantic relationships in two key ways. First, friendships provide a context in which romantic relationships can emerge. A cross-sex peer group provides opportunities to meet romantic interests. Second, adolescents learn the skills that they will need for romantic relationships from interacting in their same-sex friendships. The context of the peer group begins to shift from same-sex to mixed-sex and finally to romantic relationships during adolescence. Many of adolescents' first romantic partners emerge from their peer group. Skills that we develop in our friendships, such as cooperation, collaboration, and problem-solving, are also important in romantic relationships. Once adolescents begin to develop romantic relationships, this does not mean that they replace friendships. Instead, both friendships and romantic relationships become important.

Finally, very similar to the overall value of friendship and what it provides us, friendship remains important for our psychological well-being during adolescence. It is possible that friendship actually becomes even more important for our psychological adjustment during this developmental period due to the value placed on intimacy and self-disclosure.

There is no doubt that having at least one friend can protect us against loneliness and in turn against the development of symptoms of depression and anxiety.

16. Is it possible to have the "wrong" friends or "bad" friends?

We have discussed why friendship is so important for our well-being and many of the benefits that friendship can provide you. For instance, research has demonstrated that those who have strong friendships experience less stress, recover more quickly from heart attacks, are less susceptible to the common cold, and live longer than people who do not have friends. However, not all friendships are created equally, and in fact, not all friendships are actually beneficial. Some people have friends who lie to them, betray them, insult them, or are overly needy. Unfortunately, research into how friendship might be harmful to us is just beginning. So, in what ways might friends be bad for you? When friendships support antisocial behavior, this can be problematic and detrimental to both people involved (and potentially others). Betrayal is also bad for friendship and for the individuals involved. This could also take the form of having an affair with a friend's romantic partner. In addition, if one friend pulls away from another friend suddenly and without explanation, this can be really challenging. There may be times, however, when this is appropriate. (See Question 30 for more information on this topic.) Another type of bad friendship is when someone insults the other person. Emotional abuse can also take place within friendships. Other types of "bad" friendships include friends who lie, who are overly dependent, who never listen, who meddle too much in a friend's life, the friend who is always competing with you, and the loner who prefers not to spend time with friends. The most common type of a bad friend, though, is the promise breaker. This friend might ask you to get together for coffee, but something always comes up at the last minute and they are always canceling on you. Importantly, it may take time to realize that there is something important that you dislike about a friend. In romantic relationships, it can take 18–24 months to realize the relationship may not be right, but in friendships, this may take even longer to realize.

There are some warning signs that you could be in a bad friendship. Some people may be more interested in climbing the social ladder than truly being your friend. If someone takes a sudden interest in you out of the blue, it's good to think about why. Friendships should also always be genuine. If someone provides you with a gift that seems too expensive or inappropriate for the occasion, this is also something that you should note. It might be possible that this person is trying too hard to be your friend. Of course, true friends do not have to win you over with expensive gifts. It is the thought that counts. If a friend that you are just getting to know seems overly interested in your life, asks too many questions, or tries to imitate you to gain closer access, you might want to think twice about their friendship too. It is possible that this person is unhappy and may be copying you to try to be more like you or to steal your happiness. Watch out too for the friend who talks behind your back. Perhaps they are nice to your face, but you then hear that they are talking about you behind your back. In this case, they are revealing their true character to you. Many people are open and willing to get to know people quickly, but it is always good to be at least a little guarded in a new friendship. You should truly get to know new friends well, which takes time. The relationships will flourish and build over time. Importantly, remember that having a few close friends is much more beneficial for your well-being than accumulating hundreds of friends. Having fewer, but deeper, more meaningful connections is most valuable. Finally, it is important to trust your intuition. If something feels off with a friend or perhaps they make you feel uncomfortable, for whatever reason, trust your gut. It is often right.

So, if you determine that you do have a bad friend, how do you decide whether the friendship is worth salvaging? This will typically depend on how bad the damage to the friendship has been. Sometimes it is worth being mature and just letting whatever transpired go, but at other times, this just isn't possible or shouldn't happen (in the case of an abusive friendship). Forgiving and accepting differences with a friend will likely come easier than with a romantic partner since people typically have multiple friends and do not rely on just one friend for all of their emotional support. But if the friendship has deteriorated to the point where it is causing undue stress or one friend truly dislikes the other, it may be best to pull away from the friendship. It is best to pay attention to friendships and have them in order when life is going well and you are healthy. Unfortunately, when a crisis hits, people tend to discover just how crucial good friendship is.

17. What is co-rumination, and how can it be bad for you?

A sizeable percentage of adolescents experience clinical levels of depression (around 20 percent) or anxiety (around 10 percent), and girls are more likely to be impacted by depression and anxiety than are boys. Since girls tend to have closer friendships than boys, and we know that close relationships can protect against emotional difficulties, you might expect that girls' friendships would serve as a buffer against internalizing difficulties. However, that does not seem to be the case. One explanation that has been used to explain this contradiction in recent years is a phenomenon called co-rumination. Co-rumination refers to excessively discussing personal problems within a dyadic relationship. It includes frequently discussing problems, discussing the same problem repeatedly, mutual encouragement of discussing problems, speculating about problems, and focusing on negative feelings. Importantly, although friendship research literature indicates that self-disclosure leads to close relationships, the coping research literature indicates that dwelling on negative topics leads to emotional difficulties. As such, co-rumination links together both of these theoretical perspectives, and it has been found to be related to both positive friendship adjustment and difficulties with emotional adjustment.

Specifically, in the first research study to investigate co-rumination, third-, fifth-, seventh-, and ninth-grade participants responded to a series of questionnaires. Results indicated that co-rumination was related to high-quality, close friendships. In addition, co-rumination was related to aspects of depression and anxiety. Girls reported co-ruminating more than did boys. Importantly, self-disclosure was not related to internalizing symptoms, while co-rumination was related to internalizing symptoms. This is likely because co-rumination is an extreme and negatively focused form of self-disclosure. Subsequent studies have provided additional support for this model. Co-rumination has been found to be related to depression concurrently (i.e., at the same time) and predicts depression onset in the future.

Most recently, some researchers conducted a meta-analysis (i.e., a review of a large number of studies on a topic) exploring the relationship between co-rumination and internalizing problems. The meta-analysis also looked at moderators (i.e., constructs that might impact the relationship) between co-rumination and internalizing symptoms. Results indicated that there is a small to moderate association between co-rumination and internalizing problems. However, the size of effects between co-rumination and internalizing problems has been found to be moderate to large for children and adolescents, specifically. Findings also indicated that the size of the effect did not differ significantly across the measures of internalizing symptoms used (i.e., depression, anxiety, or a combined measure of depression and anxiety). Effect sizes also did not differ by participant age or gender. However, previous research has found that co-rumination increased the risk of depression for adolescents but not for children. Co-rumination in same-sex friendships seems to be more problematic than co-rumination in cross-sex friendships. Furthermore, consistent with prior research, results indicated that women did report higher rates of co-rumination than did men. This may be due to higher rates of self-disclosure in female friendships, which allow for more opportunities for co-rumination. The impact of co-rumination on men and women did not, however, differ. As such, if a relationship is high in co-rumination, it may have a similar negative impact for both women and men.

Thus, it appears that co-rumination can have negative impacts on an individual's psychological well-being and that these effects may outweigh the positive benefit of friendship closeness. So, how might we be able to help those who have high levels of co-rumination in their friendships, which puts them at risk for internalizing difficulties? Since engaging in repetitive, unproductive problem-focused discussions within close relationships might promote internalizing difficulties, clinical intervention can focus on these areas. Specifically, clinical intervention might focus on interpersonal strategies that those who have anxiety or depression use to manage distressing situations and help those with affective distress to consider that the ways in which they currently deal with problems may be counterproductive.

18. Is peer pressure always bad?

When we think of peer pressure during adolescence and young adulthood, it nearly always has a negative connotation. For instance, parents might be concerned about the negative influences that the peer group could have on their daughter or son. Some of this concern was based on research looking at the impact that peers have during adolescence and early adulthood that found that you are more likely to take risks in the presence of your friends. However, more recent research has told us that the relationship is not so simple and that peer pressure may in fact even be positive, at times.

In one study, the brains of 40 adolescents and adults were scanned using functional magnetic resonance imaging (MRI) while playing a virtual driving game. The game was designed to test whether players would apply the brakes at a yellow light or speed through the intersection. Results indicated that the brains of teenagers, and not the brains of adults, showed greater activity in two regions associated with rewards: the ventral striatum and the orbitofrontal cortex, when they were being observed by same-age peers than when they were playing the game alone.

This implies that rewards are more intense for teenagers when they are in the presence of their peers. Most recently, these same researchers used a computerized version of a card game to examine how the presence of peers affects the way young people gather and apply information. The computer would indicate a card from one of four decks and players could decide to either reveal or pass that card. Two of the decks would lead to a loss, and two of the decks would lead to a gain. The experimenters told the players that some decks were good and some decks were bad, but they did not tell the players which were which. Over the course of playing the game, the participants gradually figured out which decks would yield a good return. Again, teens either played the game alone or in the presence of their friends. Results showed that when peers were present, adolescents engaged in more exploratory behavior, learned faster from both positive and negative outcomes, and achieved better performance than those who played alone. This suggests that adolescents learn more quickly and effectively with their peers. Since it appears that adolescents' brains are wired to think socially, it has been argued that educators could take advantage of this. Thus, these studies indicate both the negative and positive potential of peer pressure.

Also, teens may use peer pressure to influence one another in a more intentional positive way. When teenagers make healthy choices in the friends that they choose to associate with, these friends will likely inspire them to try positive new things and to try their best. A few examples of positive peer pressure might include friends telling you to study hard so that you can get a good grade on an exam. As a result, you decide to study because it's cool to get a good grade on your test. Similarly, a group of friends all get after-school jobs, and then they convince you that you should try to get a job too in order to save money. Or several of your friends have their own cars, and this motivates you to save money so that you can buy your own car as well. So, peer pressure can be positive in several ways. First, peers can inspire you to make positive choices. Second, they might encourage you to pick up healthy habits. They may eat healthy, exercise, or abstain from using alcohol and drugs. They might also inspire you to give up bad habits. Next, peers can be there to share new experiences with you that take courage and confidence. Peers can also offer moral support through the ups and downs of life and help you to solve conflicts together. Finally, social media can also be a positive force among peers. This provides a space to run ideas by one another and a place to garner support.

If you are faced with negative peer pressure, do not panic. Here are some ideas to help you through this challenging situation. First, listen to your instincts. If you feel uncomfortable, it means that the situation is wrong for you. You can also plan for situations where you think that you might be subject to peer pressure. For instance, if you want to go to a party but you think there might be drinking or drug use taking place there, think about how you would handle this situation in advance. Think about what you would say or do in this situation. You could also arrange a "bail-out" code phrase that you could use with your parents, roommate, or a good friend whom only the two of you know. If you get into a situation where you do not feel comfortable, you can call this person and tell them your code phrase so that they can come to get you. Also, learn to get comfortable in saying no. If you are spending time with good friends, they will respect your decision, even if they don't agree with it. Do your best to spend time with people who feel similar to you in their morals. Hopefully, you will choose friends who will speak up for you when you need moral support and be quick to support you. If you are a teenager, you could also always try blaming your parents as an excuse. "Are you kidding me? My parents would kill me if they found out I did that." Finally, if a situation feels dangerous, don't hesitate to contact an adult to get help. There is no shame in reaching out for help.

What to Do as a Friend

19. How can you make friends?

To some, making new friends may seem like a simple concept. When you are a young child, you each have a toy. A peer finds it interesting; they ask you to play, and boom, you have an instant friend. You both like to play with cars, dolls, or four square at recess; boom, you're instant friends. However, as we get older, it doesn't seem so simple to make friends. By early adulthood, the prefrontal cortex of the brain is nearly fully developed, and with this development, we become more concerned about judgments made about us by others. Many adults also state that there seem to be fewer opportunities to make friends as they get older, but it's possible that this may simply be a misperception on our parts. Notably, having friends remains important during adulthood and may in fact become even more important as we age. Women and men who have 10 or more friends at age 45 reported having a significantly higher level of psychological well-being at age 50 than those who had fewer friends. Moreover, among older adults, friendship quality is predictive of good health more so than the quality of any other relationship. It appears that friendship may even impact life expectancy. People who have larger social circles have a 50 percent lower mortality risk than those who do not have a large social circle. In fact, friendship bonds have been found to be critical to maintaining both physical and emotional health. Friendship boosts the immune system, increases longevity, decreases the risk of contracting certain chronic illnesses, and increases the ability to deal with chronic pain. Poor quality social support has been found to have the monthly mortality risk equivalent of smoking 15 cigarettes per day! On the flip side, supportive friendships in your 20s are a solid predictor of being alive at age 70. High-quality friendship also reduces the risk for developing depression, post-traumatic stress disorder, anxiety disorders, and substance abuse. It is estimated that 42.6 million Americans over the age of 45 suffer from chronic loneliness, which significantly increases the risk for premature death. Some researchers have even called the loneliness epidemic a greater health threat than obesity. So, clearly making and having friends during adulthood is really important.

So, if it does seem to you that it has become harder to make friends as you have gotten older, you are not alone. However, there are some common, practical things that you can do to help ease the process. First, think about what it is you want in a friend. What kind of person would you like to hang out with? What was it about your childhood friendships that made them so special? What kinds of activities would you love to have a partner for? What kind of person fits well with your personality? If you begin by asking yourself these questions, you may be able to get a sense of just who it is that you'd like to befriend. Next, think about the existing opportunities that you do have in your life where you may be able to make friends. Are you in school? Do you have a job? Are you involved with any activities, sports, clubs, or organizations? All of these settings offer ample opportunities to meet new people with whom you already have something in common. Finding a friend or friends at work might also make you a better employee. Research has found that women who have a best friend at work are more engaged employees. Also, if you are motivated to make new friends, be sure to make time for friendship in your schedule. If you have identified someone whom you think you may be interested in getting to know better, be certain to reach out to them. Send them a text or email to set up a time to go for coffee or to take a walk. Think about how you would feel if you were to receive a message from someone new asking you to do something. More than likely you will feel flattered and more than happy to oblige.

If you're finding it challenging to meet new people, here are some suggestions to make this process a bit simpler. Challenge yourself to start up a conversation with one or two new people a day for a week. This may sound strange, but the more practice you have starting up conversations, the more natural it will become over time. You might be thinking, OK, fine, but what could I possibly talk to a stranger about? If it seems difficult to come up with questions on the spot, feel free to brainstorm some questions you could ask in advance and perhaps even practice. Some simple ways to start up conversation with others include introducing yourself and asking a question. "Do you know of any good restaurants around here?" "What kind of music do you like?" "What is your favorite TV show or movie?" "What kind of things do you enjoy doing for fun?" Make a comment about the weather, or what you watched on TV last night; practically anything can be a conversation starter. You can always lead with just one or two questions as you don't want to overwhelm your new conversation partner with questions. Also, save really personal questions for when you know them better. Once you ask a question, really listen to their answer. In general, people really do enjoy talking about themselves to someone who shows interest in them. This will also give you the opportunity to determine whether you have things in common with them and whether you want to invest more effort and time in establishing a friendship. Following the initial conversation, be sure to greet this acquaintance each time you see them. Smile, say "hi," and make small talk. All relationships, and new relationships in particular, require effort and encouragement. With a little energy and reinforcement, a newfound acquaintance can turn into a wonderful, meaningful friendship that enriches your life.

If you have just read this and thought, nope, there is no way I'm doing that or this won't work for me, try not to get too discouraged. You may need to build up inner strength to make this happen. If you believe in yourself and feel empowered, you will be able to do this. Just be yourself and you may be surprised at what you are capable of accomplishing. Remind yourself of your positive qualities and the outcome that you desire. "I'm fun to be around." "I've made friends in the past and I can do it again." "People tell me that I have a good sense of humor." "I am a thoughtful person and anyone would be lucky to be called my friend." Consider writing these things down so that you can look back at them when you feel like you are lacking in confidence. Also, don't feel as if you have to rush to make friends. It is normal for it to take time to build meaningful friendships. If you put in the time and effort, quality friendship will be the end result. If you talk to someone new and you just don't click, that is OK too, and it is to be expected. The next person you talk to may just be your future friend. In addition, if you meet someone and initially it seems like a great fit, but over time you realize it just doesn't feel right; that is OK too.

Once you've met someone who you think you'd like to get to know better, it can help to build rapport by sharing something more personal about yourself with them. Divulging something that not everyone knows to a new companion can help to build trust. You may find, in turn, that they begin to open up to you as well. Most importantly, be a good listener.

Show that you are listening by making eye contact, nodding your head, and asking a question or two about what they are saying to you. Really hear what the other person is saying and refer back to things that they told you at a later date so they know that you heard them and really truly listened. This too can help build trust and shows that you value who they are and what they have to say. In addition, if you like something about the person, share that with them. When you notice something that you like about someone and share it with them, this can be a great way to forge a connection and to start a conversation. Everyone likes receiving a compliment. However, be sure that you are being genuine in your compliments. Finally, laugh! When you let someone else know that you think they are funny, this makes them feel good about themselves and shows them that you're interested in what they have to say. It also shows that you too have a good sense of humor. If the conversation is going well, don't hesitate to ask for their phone number or email and then follow up to make plans to hang out.

Another good way to get to meet new people is to unplug. Put away your phone, your computer, your tablet, or any other electronic device. If you have your head buried constantly checking text messages, voicemails, and email, you are giving others the impression that you are unavailable and that you aren't interested in making friends. When you put away your devices and look around, you may be surprised at what you notice. You'll be much more apt to find potential new connections when you do so.

Now that you have some practical tips for starting those initial conversations to meet new potential friends, let's talk about where you might make this happen. A good step is to get involved. Some of the best places to meet people is by becoming involved in extracurricular activities (sports, clubs, youth groups, civic organizations, and book clubs, for example). Look into the clubs and activities available in your area or at your school. When you find activities that you enjoy, you'll already have something in common with people, and it gives you both something to talk about. Clubs, teams, and other groups work toward common goals, which is inspiring and can teach you how to solve problems, which helps you to bond with others. Another great way to meet new people is by volunteering. Not only do you get to meet others, you also get to feel good while doing so by making a difference in others' lives. Volunteering can be fulfilling and looks good to potential employers and schools as well. There are a multitude of places you can volunteer, including in the community, at school, or through a religious organization. You could tutor younger students, help at a food pantry, volunteer at an animal shelter, or volunteer at a hospital, just to name a few places. Nonprofit organizations are always looking for volunteers. If you are a student, consider forming a study group. You could always pass around a sign-up sheet before or after class. When you meet, you can share notes from class, study for an exam, and chat about class. You can bond over what you love about your instructor/teacher or what you despise. You can also bring snacks (who doesn't like food?) and chat about what's going on in your life. Before long, you'll find yourself building friendships. Finally, if you have a job or are interested in getting a job, this can be a great place to meet people. At jobs, you are often working toward a common goal, and you'll have something to complain or bond over with others.

No matter where, when, how, or how long it takes to make a new friend, be sure to give yourself plenty of credit for your efforts. Building and maintaining relationships is hard work, and it takes effort. Just like anything worthwhile and that you work hard at, you'll find in time that you've made new connections and that meeting new people gets easier over time. You'll be on your way to new friendships in no time.

20. What are the best ways to maintain friendships?

As adults, we have to work hard to cultivate new friendships, but it is just as important to put in the effort necessary to maintain those relationships over time. Recent research has found that the maximum number of social connections that both men and women have occurs around age 25, but as young adults begin to settle into careers, prioritize romantic relationships, and begin families of their own, their social circles tend to rapidly shrink, and friendships often take a backseat to other responsibilities and relationships. However, as we have already discussed, loneliness can be extremely problematic for both emotional and physical well-being, so maintaining friendships is imperative. There are many, many approaches to maintaining friendship, and several will be discussed here in turn.

One important way to maintain friendships is to be clear in your communication regarding your expectations. We all get busy and at times are unable to give as much to our friendships. If you are clear and upfront about this with your friends, it can go a long way. Often, if you are unavailable to your friends, they might begin to think that you are unreliable and do not value their relationship. Instead, you should be clear about your limits: "I have nearly all my classes and work on Tuesdays and Thursday this semester, so it's really hard for me to get back to you or get together on those days." "I am going to be swamped for the next couple of weeks, but I can't wait to get together once this deadline passes." "I'm really stressed right now since my Dad is sick and it's making it hard for me to focus on anything besides school." Whenever possible, be clear about how long you expect to be off the radar, whether there is a good way to communicate with you during that time, and when you expect your schedule to lighten up again. We've all heard it before and we've all said it, "I'm too busy." But you've probably also thought: "Are they really too busy or do they just not care enough to make time for me?" When we hear from others that they are too busy, we can feel like we are getting blown off. When someone says they are too busy, it isn't clear whether it is actually true or if it is their way of not really valuing your time and friendship. If someone is repeatedly saying they are too busy for you, this can signal the end of a friendship. This doesn't mean though that there was something inherently wrong with the relationship; both parties need to be willing to put in the effort to maintain the friendship. It is true that we can be really busy, so how should you handle this? Be as clear as possible about your schedule. "I'm really busy with classes till the end of December." "I've been working double shifts because work is short staffed. They are supposed to hire new employees by the end of the month." Providing your friend with context will contribute to understanding. If you're too busy to get together, suggest a phone date or video chat to maintain connection.

If you find that you are one of those people always telling your friends that you are too busy to get together, it is important to take a look at how you are spending your time. Are you checking Facebook and Instagram hundreds of times a day? Are you binge-watching TV shows on Netflix? No matter how busy you think you truly are, it is possible to make time for your friends. If you're really not sure where all of your time is going, it can be helpful to make a schedule/spreadsheet to track how your time is spent for half-hour increments for a week. This can be really eye opening with regard to providing insight into how you can make time for your friends and also how you might be able to make time for yourself to recharge. This exercise can also help you recognize where you might need to make positive, thoughtful changes in your commitments.

Another way to strengthen and maintain strong friendships in relatively little time is to engage in small, personal gestures. This can be something as simple as a brief text message, where you check in to ask, "How was that big exam in biology?" "How was your doctor's appointment?" When you remember even smaller events in your friend's life, this will show that you care. You can also send brief messages to share small amounts of information about your own day. "I finally had a chance to try that restaurant you recommended. It was really good!" "I think I did well on the psychology exam. I guess all our studying paid off!" Similarly, take an interest in what your friend is interested in these days. Maybe you think you'd hate the television show they've been watching on Netflix, but give it a try. Even if you don't really like it, you'll learn more about your friend, and they will appreciate that you tried.

It is also very important to be honest with your friends. Do your best to receive feedback from your friends without passing judgment or having your ego bruised. Expect your friends to ask you the difficult questions, and you can ask these questions of your friends in return. "Why do you think you like him or her?" "Do you think that it might actually be your fault and not theirs?" When our friends are straightforward with us, it helps us to get to know ourselves better and strengthens our relationships. So, what if we mess up in our friendships? It is important to be honest and acknowledge this and work to repair whatever has transpired. We have all had times in our lives where we have said things that we regret, but how you handle this after it occurs is most important. Be certain to set aside pride and apologize to your friend. Try to make sure that your friend understands that it was not your intention to hurt them. Be the bigger person and reach out if you know that things seem off between the two of you.

Just like anything else in your life, scheduling regular get-togethers with friends can be a really good way to ensure that not too much time passes between seeing one another. If going to coffee, watching a movie, or grabbing lunch is already marked on your calendar in regular intervals, you are much more likely to follow through with it. This doesn't necessarily have to mean that you schedule a time to see one another once a week; particularly with friends who live far away, this might mean having an annual or semi-annual get-together. Similarly, you can increase the likelihood of seeing friends if you combine this with something else that you do, such as exercising or volunteering. Plus, going to yoga class or volunteering at the animal shelter with a buddy makes it that much more enjoyable and may increase the likelihood that you'll follow through (built-in accountability)! Moreover, when you are with your friend, make sure to do your best to be fully there. Really listen to what they are saying, ask questions, and be engaged. Put away your phone and really try to focus on your friend.

This may sound like a no-brainer, but be the person who comes through for their friends. If your best friend has a graduation across the country, is getting married in another state, or their parent passes away, be the friend who finds a way to make it happen and shows up to be there with them. It won't soon be forgotten if you show up for your friend at an important event in his or her life. If you just are not able to be there, small gestures can still go a long way. Send your friend a special card, flowers, or another small token to show that you care and wish that you could be there. Similarly, be the support system for your friend even when it's not convenient for you. If they break up with their significant other at 12:30 a.m., show up at their house with cookies and let them vent. Your support will not go unnoticed. On the other hand, it is also equally important to acknowledge the efforts made by your friend. When he or she shows up for you, be sure to tell them how much it means to you that they could be there for you and what a good friend they are. Similarly, be sure to acknowledge the efforts your friend makes to check in with you and connect. Make sure that you show gratitude to your friends for what they do for you. This can be one of the keys to a happy relationship. When you acknowledge your friend, try to engage in acts of kindness and consideration that they would perceive as caring. Think about their interests and passions when you decide what to do. It is also important that both friends are putting in relatively the same amount of effort into the relationship. There will be times when you'll contribute more and other times when your friend will contribute more, depending on life circumstances, but generally contributions should be similar. If the balance of contributions seems to be out of line, be sure to discuss this with your friend. "I'm really sorry I've been more out of touch lately. I've just been really swamped with starting this new job." When people are acknowledged, their feelings are more likely to feel validated.

One might think that having a good friend or two is not enough and that you have to be popular and have lots of friends. Although this misconception is perpetuated during childhood, having even one close reciprocated friendship can be protective. It may seem that we have more "friends" today as you add your 500th Facebook friend or Instagram follower, but researchers are finding that people are actually lonelier than ever. It might be that social media is one of the reasons we spend more time on superficial friendships rather than on deep, meaningful close friendships. So, be sure to cultivate and maintain those in-person connections, and again, consider stepping away from the computer.

Just like any other important relationships in your life, your friendships will undergo transitions over time. You may move away to go off to college or start your career in a new state. It is only natural that your friendships will undergo a period of transition when your friends are no longer in immediate proximity, and you find yourself in a new location where you are adjusting and likely cultivating new relationships. If you ride out those transitions by trying to maintain your previously strong friendships while working to make new friends (see Question 19), you will fare well.

When thinking about maintaining strong friendships, try to take care more about doing what is right than about being right. When we know someone really well, we know about not only all of their good traits but also all of their bad traits. As such, it can become easy to become cynical about the negative aspects of your friend's personality. Rather than being cynical, you should do your best to demonstrate compassion. Research has shown that even children as young as two years old get joy from seeing other people being helped. When we are compassionate, that in itself can be a reward, which can leave us feeling positive regardless of how our friend is behaving. This can be another mark of a really good friend.

Another important thing that you can do for your friends is making sure that you notice if something might not seem quite right with them. You may notice that your friend is looking really tired like they are not sleeping, see a change in their hygiene, their weight is fluctuating, they are not showing up to work or class, or their house is a total mess when it's usually neat and tidy. It might be something small, but if you think something is wrong, be the one to offer to help them.

Perhaps just as important as maintaining strong relationships is knowing when to end a friendship (see Question 29 for more information). Do you feel as if there is a long-standing pattern of stress, imbalance, or resentment in your friendship? Have you begun to dread spending time with your friend, or do you feel really drained when you come home from spending time with them? Do you not like who you are when you're with this friend? These may be signs that it is an unhealthy relationship that you should end. We may feel guilty, afraid, or just out of habit stay in bad friendships longer than we should. If you end an unhealthy friendship, this will allow more time for positive fulfilling friendships. One researcher has described three areas to measure and evaluate how functional a friendship is: positivity (laughter, affirmation, gratitude, acts of service), consistency, and vulnerability. I wish you strong friendships characterized by positivity, consistency, and vulnerability.

21. Is it ever acceptable to break a friend's trust?

It is something very special for a friend to trust you enough to share a secret with you. According to research, at any given time we keep an average of 17 secrets that have been confided in us. However, newer research has indicated that being told secrets can take a toll on our mental health. When we are keeping our own secrets, we can feel burdened and weighed down, and it turns out that keeping our friends' secrets can make us feel a similar way. A research study on secret keeping, in which more than 600 participants were interviewed, showed that there are significant relationship benefits of being trusted with a secret, as well as negative impacts. It seems that the significance of the secret is important in the burden that we feel more so than what the secret is about. In particular, the greater the level of confidentiality required, the greater the impact there will be on the secret keeper. Understanding who knows, who doesn't know, and how to guard the secret can be socially and personally taxing. It seems that keeping secrets weighs on us most when we are alone. When we are alone, we start thinking about the secret, what it means, whether or not the secret might get out, and how we can cope with the information moving forward. However, there is also a positive side to being trusted with our friend's secrets. When a friend shares a secret with us, this can make us feel closer to them, and it can provide us with a sense of privilege in being viewed as someone who is trustworthy. Research has also revealed that people who are viewed as empathetic, compassionate, and assertive are most likely to be entrusted with others' secrets.

So now that your good friend has entrusted you with their secret, you are worried this isn't or shouldn't be a secret that you should keep. How will you know and what should you do in this instance? The single biggest reason not to keep a secret is if someone is being hurt, is in danger of being hurt, or when someone is potentially in danger of hurting someone else. In these instances, even though your friend will be upset that you shared their secret, it is absolutely necessary to do so. You can share the secret with a school counselor, school administrator, the college counseling center, a parent, or other trusted adult. Another secret that you should likely consider telling is if the secret would really hurt someone else. For example, if your friend tells you that your other friend's boyfriend is cheating on her but that you can't tell anyone, what do you do? You know that this would really hurt your other friend, but staying in a relationship with her boyfriend and keeping this secret from her could also be really detrimental in the long run. In this case, you can discuss the secret with the friend who told you and tell them why you think it is so important to tell your other friend and to see if you can get them on board with sharing with the friend. If your friend is still steadfast about keeping the secret, I'd recommend thinking about it for a little while, and if you still feel strongly about sharing, then move forward with telling your friend. As hard a secret this is to share, it will likely benefit her in the long run. Other secrets that you shouldn't keep include when someone reveals to you suicidal thoughts or plans, if your friend mentions to you that they are engaging in self-harm or show signs of self-harm, if there are concerns of any physical or sexual abuse or sexual assault, or you are concerned about a drug problem or addiction. In these instances, safety is the number-one priority, so these cannot be kept secret. Although you are breaking your friend's trust and they will likely be angry or upset, it is necessary to do so. They will likely move past this and perhaps even thank you one day. Know that it does not make you a bad friend if you have to break a friend's trust, in these instances.

If you encounter a secret that you know that you just cannot keep, there are ways to tactfully address this with your friend. First, let them know that you are here for them and happy to talk to them at any time. You can also let your friend know that you do not judge them and accept them no matter what. Let them know if you are concerned and that you want to get them help, if this is warranted. We all go through challenging times, but getting help and allowing others to support us can be really helpful.

22. What should you do if you think a friend has betrayed your trust?

When you open up to your friends and tell them your deepest of darkest secrets, finding out that a friend has betrayed that trust can be devastating. It can be very difficult to move on from the hurt that one can feel when their friend betrays them, but if you decide you would like to make another go at the relationship, there are practical steps you can take to try to rebuild trust and subsequently your relationship.

You can begin by clarifying the situation. You can start to do this by making sure that your interpretation of the situation is the same as your friend's interpretation. For example, you feel betrayed by your best friend, who has been your friend since kindergarten, because she has stopped returning your calls and texts, and you assume that your friendship must be over. As a result, you feel incredibly hurt and angry. However, if you don't check in with her, you would never know that your friend is actually in the midst of a deep depression and is just not able to handle anything additional right now. Sometimes things may be very different from what they seem. Additionally, it is possible that your friend does not know how sensitive the information they shared was to you. Maybe they are someone who very freely share the details of their own life and thus do not realize that this would be a big deal to you. It can always be beneficial to give someone the benefit of the doubt and to talk it through with them before making any assumptions. When you talk to your friend, this will give you the opportunity to let them know just how serious this is to you. Be sure to really hear out your friend and try to understand their perspective as well. Determining whether or not your friend meant any harm can be informative. It means something quite different if your friend lets a secret slip out by mistake versus telling your secret to intentionally hurt you. When you have a conversation with your friend, be sure to use "I feel" statements rather than "You did" or "You made me feel." This will likely lead to greater success in the conversation, and your friend will be less likely to shut down and will open up to you about his or her perspective.

Next, know that it is OK to feel whatever it is you are feeling. You need to accept and process your own feelings about the situation. Once you do so, you will begin to be able to really process your emotions. As you go through the process of understanding and accepting your emotions, they may change over time. You may start out as hurt and ultimately become angry or vice versa. The most important thing is to be honest with yourself and perhaps confide in a close other to help them understand where you are coming from and so that you can receive their support during this difficult time. It can also be beneficial to decide whether or not you want to process your feelings with the friend who hurt you. It is possible that talking through what happened with that friend may be healing. If you don't feel that you can talk to your friend about it, that is OK too, and you may decide that you want to do so at a later time.

Once you have had the opportunity to adequately process your own feelings, you will need to come to a decision about whether or not you want to remain friends. It is OK take time to sort out your feelings, and whatever decision you come to can be the right decision for you. This is a really difficult decision and one that you may feel guilty about if you decide that ending the friendship is the right thing for you to do. If you decide that you do not think you can salvage the friendship and that you want to move on, sometimes that can actually be freeing. If you believe that your friend told your secret because they wanted to embarrass or hurt you, then it makes sense to reevaluate the friendship. Even if you ultimately decide that you do not think the friendship can be repaired, it can still be useful to forgive your friend in order to free yourself and move on from the hurt and pain. When you really process your feelings, it can make a positive difference. Anger and grief that fester can negatively impact your mental health in the long run. Research has found that forgiveness lowers blood pressure and stress after an incident of betrayal and conflict. Conversely, those who held on to negative emotions associated with the initial betrayal showed the highest levels of cardiovascular reactivity and the poorest recovery patterns. Also, once you decide to end the friendship, don't beat yourself up about it or regret your decision. Any poor behavior is a reflection of your friend and not you. Be sure to allow yourself time to grieve the loss of the relationship and then try to move on to meet new people. One thing that can be really helpful is spending time with people who support and care about you or meeting new people who can begin to provide you with that support.

On the other hand, deciding to forgive your friend can also be empowering and freeing. Maybe your friend has been having a rough time lately, and they said what they did to try to make themselves feel better, or if you've been having some difficulties in your friendship, you might decide you want to work on the relationship. It is still OK to feel hurt and betrayed. If you decide you want to try to salvage the friendship, you will likely need to have a serious heart to heart, and your friend will have to be able to rebuild your trust over time. If you find that you miss your friend, you may be willing to accept him or her for who they are. If you do decide to remain friends, do not expect that things will immediately go back to the way they once were. It will likely take time for you to truly forgive and rebuild trust in your relationship. It is possible that a friendship can eventually end up stronger after a betrayal, but this will of course take time. It is also OK to let your friend know that you want to take things slowly and that it may take you some time to get back to how things used to be between the two of you. It's possible that you might feel better if other people are with you when you hang out together, you set a limit on your get-togethers (e.g., an hour for lunch), and you agree that certain topics are off-limits (e.g., if your friend gossiped about you behind your back, don't gossip about other friends). Maybe you don't want to talk for long periods of time on the phone hearing everything about their life. That is OK. Just be sure to spell out your needs as clearly as possible, and a good friend will understand or at least respect what it is you need.

23. What should you do when you disagree or fight with a friend?

In an ideal world, we would always get along with our family and friends, but in reality, we know that is simply not possible and that disagreements and fights are a part of every relationship. Conflict resolution in friendships may be even more important than in family relationships. Unlike family relationships, which we can be certain will continue for the long-term, friendships are more susceptible to potential breakdown or permanent fracture. Also, friends are invested in these voluntary relationships, so their conflict resolution skills should reflect the desire to maintain rewarding, worthwhile connections. The hallmark of a good friendship is not necessarily a lack of conflict, but rather how friends work together to reconcile after they have had a disagreement or fight. Some developmental researchers have argued that conflict resolution skills are one of the most critical determinants of friendship quality. Although there is no one right way to resolve conflict between friends, there are some strategies that researchers have identified as being adaptive and more likely to lead to reconciliation in friendship.

According to research, there are several widely used theories of conflict resolution. One of the most common is based on the "Dual Concern Model." This theory proposes that the particular conflict resolution strategy a person uses will depend upon their level of concern for themselves versus their level of concern for the other person. Collaboration, which can involve cooperation, negotiation, and compromise, occurs when there is a high level of concern for oneself and for others. This is viewed as the most adaptive form of conflict resolution. Another strategy, accommodation, is used when the concern for your friend takes precedence over your concern for yourself. This strategy can also be adaptive in some situations. Both collaboration and accommodation are viewed as solution-oriented strategies. Other less adaptive forms of conflict resolution include controlling strategies (such as hostility and coercion), which reflects more concern for the self, and nonconfrontational strategies (such as avoidance and withdrawal), which reflects a low level of concern for both yourself and others.

As you move into adolescence and then into adulthood, your ability to resolve conflicts with friends tends to increase. This is believed to occur due to an increase in perspective-taking and consideration for others. Adolescence tends to offer many opportunities to practice conflict resolution skills. Research has found that having good conflict resolution skills is associated with numerous positive outcomes. For adolescents, the strategies that they learn and practice for resolving conflict in their friendships are associated with increased friendship quality and long-term friendship maintenance. Throughout the lifetime, good conflict resolution skills have been linked to marital satisfaction and success in the workplace. In addition, research shows that the ability to successfully resolve conflict is related to empathy. Empathy is the ability to put yourself in someone else's shoes and see the situation or problem from their perspective. The ability to have empathy during conflict can be valuable. If someone is able to perceive and identify with another's distress or frustration in a conflict situation, this can lead to a better understanding of the other person's position, which may lead to the use of more effective conflict resolution strategies. For instance, one study found that adolescents who were higher in empathy were more likely to discuss issues with friends, use compromising strategies, and were less likely to become angry when resolving conflicts with friends.

Your friend blew you off. You heard that your friend gossiped behind your back. You and your friend have a huge disagreement. You find that you and your friend are drifting apart. All of these things (and so many more) can lead to conflict. So, if conflict is inevitable in your friendships and having good conflict resolution skills is so important, what are some practical things you can do to handle conflict in your friendships? There are several things that you can do to help handle conflict respectfully and tactfully in your relationships. It can be helpful to first ask yourself a number of questions in order to assess the conflict and the state of your friendship. First, is the friendship worth saving? How did I contribute to the current state of our friendship? When did the friction first start? What was happening at that time? What should I have done when I started to become emotionally distressed? What is my part in managing and resolving the conflict with my friend? Does my friend value our friendship? How can I rebuild our friendship? What should I tell my friend? What should I ask my friend?

When you decide that it's time to discuss the conflict with your friend, keep these tips in mind. Make sure that you have a good handle on your emotions before you decide to tackle a discussion about conflict. Also, take into consideration your friend's state of mind. If they are really stressed or really tired, it might not be the right time to have a heartfelt talk. Since you want to have a serious conversation, it can be helpful to let your friend know this in advance so that they do not feel caught off guard. It can also be useful to choose a time and a place to meet that you both agree upon. It might be helpful to meet in a neutral place, such as a coffee shop or restaurant. Be sure to be upfront with your friend. Explain the way you feel, why you believe there is a conflict, and how you think you can resolve it. Make sure to use "I" statements. Focus on what you are feeling and what you are thinking rather than saying "you did this" or "you made me feel." Those types of statements will likely put your friend immediately on the defensive and your perspective will be less likely to be heard. Try your best to use active listening skills. Really listening to your friend and paying attention to what they are saying is vital to managing conflict. Make good eye contact, hear your friend out, try to reflect their perspective back to them to make sure you are getting it right, and think before you respond. Then work together with your friend to jointly come up with a course of action to resolve the conflict. If you both agree upon the solution, you're much more likely to both feel good about it and follow through with the plan. If you find that discussing the conflict with your friend is not going well and things are escalating, this can be a good clue that it's time to take a break and come back to discuss the conflict at a later time once everyone has had a chance to cool off. If you remove yourself from the situation, the distance and time will likely help you (and your friend) to think more clearly about the situation and problem at hand.

When you decide to resolve a conflict with a good friend and try to work to repair your relationship, it can be important to remind yourself what your friend means to you and in turn be sure to express to your friend how much they mean to you. This can help remind your friend why the friendship is one that is worth working on fixing. Once you've had the big discussion, you both might still need a little space. The fight has likely taken an emotional toll on you both. Take the time that you need to work through your feelings and practice good self-care (take a bath, read a book, go for a walk, talk to someone else you care about and trust). Also, try your best not to let others' perspectives cloud your judgment. If you trash talk your friend to your family or a significant other, it might feel good in the moment, but it could make things uncomfortable in the future when you make up with your friend. Or, even worse, your friend could find out that you talked trash about them behind their back, and that will only harm that relationship even more.

Once you've had a fight with a friend, it's important to try to prevent similar disagreements from happening again in the future. If you find that you are repeatedly fighting with your friend, see if there are any issues that come up again and again and try to identify a solution to these issues. This might mean that you need to talk bluntly with your friend about what's going on in the relationship. There may only be a solution if the two of you work together to come up with it, so be honest and let them know that you want to avoid another fight by cooperating and working with one another to change. Try to think in broad terms and work together on moving forward. Is there an imbalance in the friendship? Is someone too critical? Does someone feel like they are making all the effort? Was someone's confidence breached? Working together to come to a compromise can be really worthwhile and can help prevent similar disputes from reoccurring in the future. Finally, no matter who was right or wrong in a fight, there is always something that you can learn from it. Arguments can bring out the worst in us and amplify our most negative personality characteristics, but they can also give us a chance to identify when we are not being our best selves and work on oneself. Arguments can also provide the opportunity to reflect on how we can be better communicators. It might be as simple as providing your friend with a warning about when you are feeling moody so that it gives them a chance to avoid potential friction. If you discover something along the way, it can make it easier not to get hung up on a fight and to move on in your relationship. Remember even when you have repaired your friendship, things may not be the same as they were previously. Your friendship will still require a lot of nurturance. Be willing to listen to new stories and adapt to changes in your friend's life (transitions to new jobs, new friends, new significant others). Work together to build new memories to continue to strengthen your relationship.

24. What can you do if you develop romantic feelings for a friend and they are not reciprocated? What can you do if your friend develops romantic feelings for you and you don't feel the same way?

At some point in time, most people will develop romantic feelings for someone who does not feel the same way about them. In one study of high school and college students, unrequited love was four times as common as reciprocated, equal love. Not surprisingly, experiencing romantic rejection after pouring your heart out to someone can cause significant pain. Some research suggests that brain activity following rejection resembles that caused by physical pain. Although this is very challenging, it may still be possible to salvage the friendship. So why might you fall for a friend or he/she fall for you? Developing romantic feelings for friends is not uncommon. Love grows over time, and friendship can provide several opportunities for intimacy to flourish. First, many people believe that a strong friendship serves as an essential foundation for a romantic relationship. In fact, some people prefer to build a friendship with someone before having a romantic relationship with them. Next, people tend to spend a lot of time with close friends, so it may become difficult to imagine not having that friend as an integral part of your life. Friendship often grows out of shared interests, and when you have a lot in common with someone, this may make them appear to be an optimal romantic partner. Some friendships may also have mixed signals. If you have a friendship that is characterized by physical affection or flirtatious jokes, it may provide the impression of mutual romantic interest. Finally, attachment style may play a role in unrequited love. If someone's primary caregiver was unpredictable with their affection or inconsistently met their needs, this can lead to an anxious/ambivalent attachment. As an adult, an individual with an anxious/ambivalent attachment style tends to be more likely to develop romantic attraction for people who are unlikely to reciprocate their romantic feelings.

Is it possible that a friendship can survive if both friends don't feel the same way about one another? Hopefully, the friend who does not have romantic feelings will apologize and let the other friend know that they just do not feel the same way but that they do value the friendship. Inevitably, the rejected party will feel sad and hurt. These feelings are normal and will pass over time. It is typical to grieve where you may feel sad, hurt, confused, or angry. Importantly, these feelings should not be taken out on the friend because neither of you can help the way that you feel. It is also normal that the friendship may feel different or awkward for a while. It may be best to not bring up the situation once you decide to remain friends and try to move on from it. Importantly though, avoiding your friend is not the way to handle the situation. Friends who continue to see one another are more likely to remain friends. Try your best to keep the lines of communication open. If, however, you are the one who developed romantic feelings and you are having a difficult time moving on from them, it may be best to step back from the friendship while you focus on healing. You may consider interacting with your friend in a group setting rather than one-on-one setting. It is also not unusual to feel a decreased sense of self-worth or lower self-esteem after experiencing romantic rejection. If talking with other friends and family does not seem to be helping, it may be worthwhile to reach out to a therapist. It is also important to put yourself and your own needs first while healing. When you feel ready, pursue other relationships. This may even mean seeking out new friends. If one wants to stay friends, there are also some things to avoid doing. First, the friend who is not romantically interested should not disclose to others that the friend revealed that they were romantically interested. Second, the friend who is not romantically interested should not invent a new love interest to justify the rejection. Finally, if the friendship was characterized by lots of physical affection or flirtation, this should be toned down so as to keep the relationship platonic.

25. How do you know if someone is a true friend?

In the age of the Internet, online friendships, and texting, it might be difficult to determine whether someone is an acquaintance, a passing friend, or destined to be a true, lifelong friend. However, there are several characteristics that genuine friends possess that can help you to differentiate between those who are destined to be true friends and those who are not. So, if you are interested in that indescribable bond or determining whether you have that bond with your friend, be sure to read the rest of this entry.

True friends not only accept you for who you are but also encourage you to truly accept yourself for who you are. If you have ever heard that we are our own worst critics, this is true. However, having close, supportive friendships can help us to feel more confident in ourselves. If we are feeling down about not doing well on a test or losing a job, real friends help you to point out your strengths and to let you know that everything will be OK. Your friends should encourage you and build you up and should not be one-upping you (e.g., "That's great that you got an 88 percent on the chemistry test; I got a 95 percent on it"). Similarly, true friends should not talk about you behind your back. If you find that your friend talks about others as soon as they leave the room, gossips about others, or is often saying negative things about others, this can be a sign of bad character and indicate that they might be doing the same thing to you when you are not around.

We can also feel better about ourselves when we are supportive of our friends in a similar manner. Our true friends understand us and what helps us to function. As such, these friends can often sense stress in one another. When we are feeling stressed, they can help us to feel calmer. We can also help our friends to feel calmer as well. Research has shown that just spending time with a best friend can help to beat stress.

Although friends pick us up when we are feeling down, they can also call us out when we are wrong. Everyone has flaws, and sometimes these flaws can cause interference in our relationships and our lives. True friends can gently point out some of these flaws to help us to improve ourselves. When you have developed a friendship where there is a high level of trust and honesty, friends are able to share what is on their minds, even when this is not always positive. This can be a really valuable part of a relationship when we have someone who can be honest with us about our strengths and also our less-than-stellar attributes. Importantly, our true friends can also help to keep us humble. They are there for us to celebrate all of our accomplishments, but they can also help ensure that we do not let these successes go to our heads. Real friends can remind you of where you started, how far you have come, and who you truly are.

Importantly, real friends are there for you. This means that they make you a priority by giving you their time and undivided attention. So, when you are with your friend, be sure to put away your phone and give him or her your full undivided attention as well. Research has found that just having your phone in front of you has the ability to take away from personal connections. Just the mere presence of a phone in the room makes one feel less connected and less close to their friend. Once friends have one another's undivided attention, they also need to really listen to one another. It is important that true friends have open, two-way dialogues with one another. True friends work hard to be good listeners who validate whatever their friend is feeling. If you find that you are always the one who is listening to your friend's problems or your friend always seems distracted when you are together (e.g., checking their phone, taking calls, asking you to repeat yourself), you might want to take a closer look at your relationship to see if it is really offering you what you want out of a friendship. Even when life gets really busy and it's easy to put friends on the back burner, genuine friends continue to show up for one another and do not let life get in the way of their friendship. This might mean that your friend carves out time to text you, lets you know that he or she is thinking about you, makes time for a phone call, or plans a visit. Not making time for friends can be one of the key reasons why friendships fail, drift apart, or end.

You may have heard that the true test of friendship is to see who is there when the going gets tough, and there is some truth to this statement. It is great to have friends who can be there for us when things are going well and we are successful, but true, genuine friends are there for one another through all of life's ups and downs. So, do pay attention to who is there for you when something bad happens to you or you are going through a difficult time. This may be a sign that this friend is there for the long haul. This should also be reciprocated. You should be there for your true friends no matter what. This means that sometimes life can get complicated or tricky. If you find out that your friend's significant other is cheating on him or her or you see their significant other flirting with someone else, it is important to share this information with your friend. Even though this is a difficult conversation to have, true friends owe one another honesty. In turn, your true friends should be honest with you too, even when this is the hard thing to do.

Even when we have true friendships, they do not always run smoothly. It is inevitable that friends will hurt one another's feelings. The key is that true friendships can weather hurt feelings. Rather than keeping hurt feelings to themselves, true friends tell one another what is bothering them. Real friends do not let tensions build and build until they explode; instead, they confront the difficulty head-on and ideally as soon as possible. Friends will appreciate honesty and have the ability to forgive one another.

Finally, true friends make us want to improve ourselves. When friends are kind, genuine, and supportive, they can serve as an example for us about who we want to be and help make us better people. It is important to think about how your friend makes you feel. If you are happy when you are around them and they make you feel good about yourself and encourage you, these are good signs you may have found a true friend.

26. What can you do if you are worried about a friend?

At one time or another, we have all likely been concerned about the emotional well-being of one of our friends. The challenging thing is knowing what to do and how to handle things when you are concerned about a friend. One thing to keep in mind is that your role is to simply be a friend. Since you care about your friend, you may feel obligated to try to do more than you are equipped to handle. Remember, you are not a mental health professional, so your role should be to support your friend and not try to diagnose them, give medical advice or treatment, make decisions for your friend, try to solve their problems, tell them to stop feeling how they do, tell them to just get over it, or minimize how they feel even if you do not understand it yourself. A great place to start is by letting your friend know that you are worried about them. It is important to tell them what it is that you are worried about and about any changes you have observed in them. It is possible that they have a different perspective and you will want to hear out what they have to say. Your friend may have a difficult time opening up about what they are experiencing, but you can still ask what you can do to help and try be a good listener. If someone is going through a challenging time with their mental health, alcohol, or drugs, just talking through their experiences can be very valuable. To be a good friend, you should do your best to listen to your friend without judgment. Try to resist the inclination to give your friend advice and just really be there to listen to them. To be an active listener, you can reflect back what your friend is saying and ask clarifying questions. If your friend is really resistant to talking, it may be best not to push the issue.

If you are concerned about your friend's mental health, this can be a good opportunity for you both to grow together. You can work together to learn more about mental health (e.g., anxiety), which may help you better understand what your friend is experiencing. This may include things like finding books or trustworthy websites and reading them together. You may also be able to find educational events or classes on mental health through a local community mental health center, school, or college campus.

Many mental health conditions, such as depression and anxiety, are very common with at least 7–18 percent of the population experiencing clinical levels of these concerns at some point in their lifetime. If you have experienced a mental health concern in the past or are currently seeking support, you have a lot of insight to offer your friend on how to deal with what they are facing and to offer ways to stay as well as possible. Opening up to your friend about similar challenges may help them to feel like they are not alone; you can empathize with their experience, and you may be able to offer practical suggestions such as a referral for a good therapist.

Other ways that you may be able to help your friend are more practical. You may offer to help them with day-to-day tasks like cooking them a meal, returning their library books, or accompanying them to an appointment. These small daily tasks can actually make a really big difference. You may also want to help your friend find help by connecting them to services, if they are open to the idea. If you are in high school, a good place to start may be your school counselor. They can meet with the student and provide recommendations for referrals in the community. Another good point of contact is a primary care physician. If you are a college student, the college counseling or wellness center can be a great resource, which typically offers free services to students. Finally, if you are concerned that your friend is in crisis, you can always call 9-1-1. You may also wish to provide your friend with a 24-hour hotline number, such as the National Suicide Prevention Lifeline (1-800-273-8255).

If you find that your friend is not ready to accept help, this can feel like a really challenging situation. Although you do not have full control over the situation, you can let your friend know that you are there for them when they are ready to talk. You should not confront your friend with problems that you have noticed, but you can let them know, "I've noticed that you've been canceling plans lately, and it makes me feel sad. Is there something going on?" If they bring up any problems to you, you can respond to them and suggest someone who may be able to help (such as the school counselor or college counseling center). Think about where you had been in the past when your friend had opened up to you—does it help to go for a walk or go out for coffee? If you are really concerned about your friend and they are not opening up to you or are not receptive to help, you can let them know that you are really worried and that you have to tell someone else. You can then tell a trusted adult like a parent, teacher, or school counselor. It is possible that your friend may be angry and feel as if you have betrayed their trust, but it is more important that they are safe.

Finally, when you are concerned about your friend's well-being, it is inevitable that this will impact you too. It is normal to feel overwhelmed or upset, and it is important to take care of your own health too. Try your best to ensure that you are eating well, getting enough sleep, exercising, and engaging in things that you enjoy. If you are having a hard time yourself, don't hesitate to get some support for yourself by talking to someone you trust or reaching out to some of the resources mentioned above.

27. What should you do if a friend is making choices that you disagree with?

If you are concerned about the choices that a friend is making, you can sometimes feel stuck or powerless in this situation. However, there are a number of things that you can do that may be helpful for your friend. First, if your friend has confided in you, then they trust you, and chances are that they are open to your input. It is important to try to be a good listener. Sometimes your friend may not realize that they are making bad decisions, and talking about things can help them process their choices. Once you have heard your friend out, provide them with some feedback and be honest. If you are concerned about a choice your friend is making, be sure to tell them and tell them why you are concerned. Talk to your friend from a loving but concerned place. If your friend is in danger, act quickly to put together a plan to help. You can provide your friend with hotline numbers. There are hotlines out there for domestic violence, suicide, substance abuse, and eating disorders. You can look up local resources online for your friend. It may also be necessary to tell or get others involved, if you are really concerned about your friend's safety. Be honest with your friend and let him or her know who you will need to tell and why. Make sure they know that you are concerned about them and want them to be OK. Let them know that you are there for them.

In particular, if you are concerned that your friend is abusing drugs, there are some clues that may tell you if this is the case. You can watch for sudden changes in your friend's behavior or mood. Your friend might begin to withdraw from family and their usual friend group. Your friend may seem to lose interest in things that they typically enjoy, such as hobbies or sports. You may notice a change in their personal hygiene or that they begin to neglect their responsibilities. There can also be physical signs that someone may be using drugs. Their eyes may be red, glassy, or bloodshot. They may be sniffling more than usual, have a runny nose, or have frequent nose bleeds. They may shake and have tremors, their speech may be slurred or incoherent, or their coordination may be impaired. You may notice that they have suddenly lost or gained weight. Other clues that your friend could be using substances include finding drug paraphernalia such as pipes, spoons, or syringes. You might find small resealable bags that could be used to store drugs or burnt foil. You may also look out for things that are missing, such as money, valuables, or prescription drugs.

If you notice some of these warning signs, you may wonder what you can do to help. This can feel daunting and overwhelming. However, it is important to try to help your friend. You will need to acknowledge that it is possible that your friend might not see their drug abuse as a problem. You should have an honest conversation with your friend and express your concerns. Be sure that you let them know that you think abusing drugs is serious. Talk to your friend about your concerns and how drug abuse impacts their friends and family. Sometimes they may not be concerned about their own health, but seeing that their behavior is negatively impacting those whom they love and care about can sometimes be powerful. Try to keep your friend focused on positive goals that do not include using drugs. Acknowledge and support positive things that they do and achieve and let your friend know that you are there for them. Whatever you do, do not try to threaten your friend, bribe them, or guilt-trip them. This will more than likely backfire and end up pushing them farther away. Sometimes no matter what you try, it may not be enough to get your friend to stop using drugs. You can provide your friend with resources that are out there to help and, if needed, talk to their family members. Also, make sure not to forget about yourself and your own emotional needs. Do your best to take care of yourself and turn to others when needed.

Along those same lines, if you are concerned that a friend is drinking too much, there are things you can do to try to help. Signs to look out for that indicate that your friend may be drinking too much include having trouble stopping drinking or controlling alcohol intake; consistently using alcohol to relax; forgetting what was happening when they drank/experiencing blackouts; lying to other people about their drinking habits; experiencing relationship, work, school, or legal problems due to drinking; and having family members or friends express concern about their drinking. When you decide that you want to approach your friend, be sure not to lecture them. Instead, share your concerns and try to do so when they are sober. It may also be helpful to talk to a doctor or mental health professional before you confront your friend about their drinking. They can provide you with realistic expectations and resources. It is common for people to become upset or deny that they have a problem, so be prepared for this. When you raise your concerns, try to be as specific as possible. Provide examples of how their drinking has caused problems and let them know that you are there to support them. Finally, remember again to take care of yourself. Seek out support to help you get through this challenging time, and remember that recovery is a process that takes time.

28. Why do friends drift apart?

There are several signs that you may be drifting apart from a friend. First, if you find that you are spending less time than you usually would with a friend, this may be a sign that your relationship is strained. You may be getting together less often or connecting over the phone or via text less frequently. Second, you may notice that you are reaching out to your friend less often. If you find that you are backing away more often, this could be increasing the distance between the two of you. You may also find that the quality of your interactions with your friend have changed. If your interactions seem to have a decidedly negative focus, this too could be a sign that something is off in your relationship. Perhaps you now find that your friend is often disappointing you, complaining to you, or even insulting you. Research has found that friendships should have a 5:1 ratio of positive to negative (comments/interactions) to remain healthy. So, strive to balance any negative comments with compliments. Next, you may be drifting apart from your friend if you find that you are refraining from telling your friend things. When relationships are strong, friends should be able to be vulnerable with one another. So, if you find that you are holding something back from your friend, especially something you would have typically told them, this may be another sign of a strained relationship. Similarly, if you feel that your friend is no longer confiding in you and holding things back, this too could be a sign that your relationship is strained. In addition, if you feel disconnected from your friend, this is a sign that you are drifting apart. We can all become disconnected from friends at times (e.g., lives are busy, etc.), but if you find that you are not connecting and you don't have the desire to reconnect, it is likely a sign that your relationship is strained. Perhaps you feel that your friend is no longer interested in your life or that you no longer feel comfortable when you do get together and you are unable to open up about your feelings to them. If you do find that when you get together you are unable to open up and feel anxious or uncomfortable (when you used to feel calm and relaxed), this too can be a sign that you are drifting apart. Sometimes nothing major has changed in your friendship, but your life circumstances have changed and your friend just no longer fits well in your life anymore. For instance, maybe you have changed jobs, are going to a new school, or have begun dating someone new.

So, you have noticed signs that you may be drifting apart from a friend, but why do you think your friendship has changed? Importantly, not all of our friends are meant to be in our lives forever. In fact, most friendships do end at some point for many different reasons. First, friends may drift apart because of sudden changes in their life (e.g., a new job, attending a new school, moving, getting married, having a baby). When these types of life changes occur, it is possible that you no longer share the same things in common. Another reason that a friendship can dwindle is due to a lack of trust. If a friend shows a lack of respect by not listening, gossiping, or talking over you, this may decrease your trust in your friend. As a result, you may be more guarded around them. Unfortunately, you cannot have a true friendship if one person feels uncomfortable and is unwilling to share their feelings because of the fear that this information will be misused. However, it is also possible that you may just grow apart from a friend and that there is no real negative reason that you are drifting apart. Perhaps the things that drew you together in the first place (e.g., being classmates) have changed, and as a result, you no longer have the same connection or things to talk about.

If you are in fact drifting apart from your friend, particularly a best friend, this can be really challenging for you. However, there are several things that you can do that might help you to deal with this transitional period in life. It can definitely take time to get over the sadness of losing a friend with whom you were once close. Importantly, when you are trying to move on from a friendship, you should do your best not to harp on the past. If you focus on the past and the mistakes that were made, this will only make you feel worse. Instead, do your best to focus on all the positive aspects of your friendship: how they helped you to grow as a person, how they supported you, and how they helped you to change. Remembering the positive impact that someone had on your life can help you to feel better and help you realize that not everyone is meant to stay in your life forever. Next, work to accept your share of blame for what transpired in the relationship. If you are able to accept why the friendship ended, this can help you to move forward in life and in your friendships. It may also help you in future relationships. While you are working to move on from a friend whom you have drifted apart from, you should try to keep yourself busy. Keeping yourself busy can also help open you up to new opportunities (e.g. new clubs, activities, sports) that allow you to build new connections and make new friends. Similarly, do your best to be open to making new friends. If you speak to and open yourself up to new people, you may find yourself connecting with someone who you never expected to connect with. You never know where you might meet a new friend. Next, try your best not to let the dissolution of this friendship impact your other friendships. For instance, don't try to spend all your time with another friend to fill the void of the friend you have lost. Finally, take time to focus on yourself. It will take time to move on from the friendship that you lost, but picking up a new hobby or healthy habit (e.g., going to the gym regularly) can be beneficial. Be patient with yourself, and you may find that you grow in the process.

29. How do you know if you should end a friendship?

As difficult as it can be to end a friendship, sometimes it is the best thing to do for your own emotional well-being. There are signs that you can look for that can provide insight it may be time to consider ending a friendship. Often you will get a feeling that a friendship just does not feel right any longer. If this is the case, do not ignore that feeling. If you find that you are pouring a lot more energy into the relationship to maintain it than your friend is, this may be a sign that it's time to end the relationship. Friendships should be mutual and not one-sided. Although there may be times when one friend temporarily gives more to the relationship than the other (e.g., your friend loses a parent, goes through a breakup, is struggling with depression), this should not be an ongoing trend in the relationship. If your friend only turns up when they are going through a hard time or they need something, this is likely a sign that it might be time to stay goodbye to your friend. Similarly, if you are always reaching out to make plans and your friend is often bailing on you, this too can be a bad sign. Friendships, like any relationship, need to be built on trust. So, if your friend has betrayed your trust once, or more than once, it may be difficult to recover from this. If the betrayal of trust was severe, such as cheating with your significant other or stealing from you, the relationship may not be worth maintaining. Similarly, if you tell your friend something in confidence and they are not able to keep your secret, this can be a red flag. It is important that you feel you can trust your friend, and so if you feel that you can't, you may not want to maintain the relationship any longer. In addition, if your friend seems to always have drama following them, you might be wise to think about whether or not this is a good relationship for you to continue. If someone always has drama happening, it can negatively impact your friendship. Sometimes these individuals' lives may be unhealthy or chaotic. If the two of you are always fighting and can't seem to resolve your disagreements, this may be a sign that it is time for the friendship to end.

There are other signs, which may not seem as obvious, that it may be time to end a friendship too. For instance, if you have a friend who is always very negative and is not making any effort to change, you may eventually want to move on from this friendship. If you are always trying to be there for your friend and cheer them up, this might ultimately bring you down. If you feel that your efforts to help are in vain, this can be draining. As we have discussed previously, sometimes friends just drift apart for various reasons. So, if you find that you don't have much to say to your friend any longer and this persists, this may be a sign that it's time for you both to move on from the friendship to new relationships. If you do want to save the friendship where you don't feel like you have much to talk about anymore, you can try talking with your friend about how your lives have changed or try to focus on a common activity that you do both enjoy. When you raise a concern that you have to a friend, they should listen to you and acknowledge your concern, even if they do not agree with you. So, if your friend dismisses you when you raise a concern (particularly if this is a pattern for them), you may want to think about whether you want to continue your relationship. Some people will turn a problem immediately back on the other person—tell you that you are wrong or that you are overreacting. Even if a friend doesn't agree with you, a good friend will hear you out and care about your feelings. Good friends should also bring out the best in us. If instead, you are spending time with your friend and they are making you feel worse rather than better, this too can be a sign that this may not be a friendship in which you should be investing your time and energy. Finally, if you find that you avoid returning your friend's calls and texts, dread spending time with them, or the time you spend together leaves you feeling more drained and negative, this can be a sign that it's time to end the friendship.

Finally, here are some questions you can ask yourself to help you decide if it might be time to end your friendship. Do you look forward to talking to your friend and spending time with them? Do you have fun when you are together? What does this friendship add to your life? Do you feel appreciated and respected by your friend? Can you count on your friend? Does your friend bring out the best in you? Do you feel like there is give and take in the relationship or do you feel like you're putting in all the effort? Have you expressed your concerns about your friendship? What have you done to try to improve your relationship? Is it possible to save your friendship?

30. In what ways can you end a friendship respectfully?

If you have decided that you do in fact want to end a friendship, there are ways to do so out of respect for your friend and the relationship that you have shared. First, let's discuss the ways in which I do not recommend ending a friendship. First, you should not just cut off all contact and no longer communicate with your friend. Also, you should work hard not to act hostile or aggressive toward your friend. You should also make sure that you don't try to take the easy way out of ending the relationship by enlisting other friends to tell the person you no longer want to be friends with them. Finally, you should not avoid having this difficult conversation face-to-face. As such, you should never end a friendship over text or in an online chat.

In contrast, there are several healthy ways to end a friendship. First, you can work to gradually reduce the social contact that you have with the friend. This may provide a natural end for the friendship over time. This may be a particularly useful way to end the relationship if you really do not want to have a confrontation with the friend or you are afraid of confrontation. This may come about if your friend has responded really negatively to being confronted in the past or did not take your concerns seriously. Gradually fading from a friendship can also help to reduce hurt feelings. If the friend reaches out to you in the process, you can take time to respond to them, provide brief responses, or just be unavailable if they ask to get together with you. Although this may seem like a kind way to end a friendship, it may drag things out and, in the end, might put your friend through more hurt feelings than are necessary.

Another way that you can end a friendship respectfully is to have a direct conversation with your friend to discuss your concerns. In order to have this conversation, you could ask your friend to get coffee, tea, or some other beverage that you both like so that you can chat. This talk should always happen face-to-face, never online or via text message. You should also be certain to have a goal for this conversation. Think about what you want to discuss and achieve during the talk. Work to begin the dialogue by saying something that will be open to conversation, for example, "I've noticed we've been having a lot of arguments in our friendship over the past couple months, and that's been bothering me. I wondered if we could talk about it." Then discuss how you are feeling rather than what you friend has done wrong. If you keep the conversation focused on your feelings and your goal, it should go OK, and your friend will be less apt to shut down. Remember to take time to listen to your friend and what they have to say as well. When you have this face-to-face conversation, be sure to admit your own mistakes, apologize for anything you feel you have done wrong, and have compassion for your friend. Think of how you would want to be treated if roles were reversed and then act this way toward them. If you determine through this conversation that you cannot resolve your differences, you may decide to take a break from the friendship. This can have positive benefits that simply ending a friendship does not. The time away from the relationship may provide you with a new perspective, gives you a chance to calm down, provides you with an opportunity to reevaluate your friendship, and gives you time to see if you miss your friend. However, if after having the conversation you decide that you want to end your friendship immediately, here are some recommendations for doing so. This may be particularly the case if the relationship has been toxic or damaging to you or the friend does not respect boundaries that you have set. When this is the case, being straightforward is best. You can let your friend know that your needs are no longer being met in the friendship and that you wish them all the best in the future. Although this can be awkward in the moment, it is clear and unambiguous. Then, once you have ended your friendship, be sure to take time for yourself to heal. Keep yourself busy and consider engaging in new activities where you may meet new people.

Current Trends in Friendship

31. Is having a friend online the same as having a friend in person?

Although research into online relationships is a relatively new field of inquiry, it has begun to examine the similarities and differences between online and face-to-face friendships. Two hypotheses have been proposed for how Internet communication might relate to adolescents' and young adults' offline social lives: the social compensation hypothesis and the rich-get-richer hypothesis. The social compensation hypothesis proposes that those who are introverted, shy, or socially anxious might benefit most from using the Internet. The Internet would allow them to behave differently than they would in their face-to-face interactions. If this were to be the case, the Internet could offer a lonely person a place to make new friends, a socially anxious person could feel comfortable without the pressures they face in in-person interactions, and a depressed young adult could use social media to express feelings and receive support in return. In contrast, the rich-get-richer hypothesis proposed that those who are socially competent, outgoing, and have positive face-to-face social relationships will benefit most from the Internet. These individuals are believed to have more social partners with whom they can interact online and are more socially comfortable. Most of the early research evidence supported the rich-get-richer hypothesis. In one of the first longitudinal studies to explore these hypotheses, researchers followed a sample of families for a year after purchasing a computer and gaining access to the Internet. For individuals that were high on extraversion, Internet usage was associated with more positive psychological adjustment, greater community engagement, higher self-esteem, decrease in negative emotion, and lower levels of loneliness. It was also associated with increased family connection and computer skills. Unfortunately, the opposite was true for those high on introversion. Their Internet usage was associated with poorer psychological health. As such, the most support has been found for the rich-get-richer hypothesis. One research study has lent support to the social compensation hypothesis. Adolescents who were high on social anxiety viewed online communication as more useful for intimate connection than those who were low on social anxiety.

The majority of research thus far has supported that there is continuity between online and offline social interactions. It seems that adolescents explore key developmental issues, such as identity and sexuality, online in the same way they do in face-to-face conversations. Similarly, face-to-face aggression and cyber aggression tend to be correlated, and prosocial behavior in offline interactions predicts prosocial behavior online. Cyber aggression is defined as behavior intended to harm another person using electronic communication that is perceived by the target as harmful. Correlations between traditional aggression and cyber aggression have been found. A large study of college students aged 18–25 completed online surveys, which included four points to assess prosocial behavior in face-to-face interactions (helping someone with a problem, being friendly to someone needing help, defending someone who is being picked on or excluded, and helping someone join a group). Participants also answered questions about similar prosocial behaviors online. Results showed that face-to-face prosocial behaviors positively correlated with prosocial communication online.

Adults may fear that adolescents' online activity and relationships may come at the expense of high-quality in-person relationships, but few studies have specifically examined this. The evidence that is available suggests that, overall, engagement with social media is positively related to high-quality relationships, especially for those high in social competence. Surveys have found a positive relationship between self-reported online communication and perceived closeness with friends and friendship quality. For girls, this relationship held regardless of social anxiety. For boys, those having higher social anxiety and who used the computer more to communicate with friends had higher-quality friendships than those having high social anxiety and who did not have as much online communication with friends. In another study, researchers look at the Facebook profiles of young adults who had previously participated in a study on their peer relations and found that the number of Facebook friends and the amount of socially supportive communication on their Facebook walls was correlated with reports of positive qualities of offline friendships. The long-term effects of online relationships remain to be found.

32. How has the Internet and social media changed friendship?

The Internet has become an integral part of adolescents' and young adults' lives. In the United States, 24 percent of teens report going online "almost constantly," and 75 percent of 12- to 17-year-olds have access to cell phones. More than 71 percent of adolescents use more than one social networking site, with 71 percent using Facebook, 52 percent using Instagram, 41 percent using Snapchat, and 33 percent using Twitter. It also seems that girls are more interested in visual social media than boys with 61 percent of girls and 44 percent of boys reporting that they use Instagram. Social media offers adolescents connection with their peer group in ways that were not previously possible.

Given this newer and important research area for peer relationships, methods to study friendship online have emerged. Self-report questionnaires are still the most common way of studying online friendships. This method is both practical and inexpensive, but it is possible that people will not report their own social media interactions accurately. It is possible that adolescents may be motivated to hide their involvement in negative activities (e.g., cyberbullying, illegal activity) or simply because they are not able to accurately recall their online activity. Self-reports can capture lurking behavior online that wouldn't be captured through directly observing an adolescent's social media profiles. Research has found that girls who passively view peers' Facebook profiles exhibit higher levels of depression than girls who engage with their peers' Facebook profiles. Another method that has been used to study peer relationships online is the experience sampling method (ESM). In ESM, participants are contacted on their cell phones via text message a set number of times in a given period of time (e.g., five times per day). Participants then respond by rating their social media usage, offline activities, and various ratings of psychological functioning since their last check-in. This methodology has enabled researchers to examine how interacting with social media relates to life satisfaction and depression in real time. Since this research method is quick and easy, it allows researchers to test short-term relationships over the course of days or weeks. The final method that has been used to study online relationships is direct observation. It is relatively easy and inexpensive to study participants' social media interaction for weeks, months, and even years. This also limits adolescents' and young adults' ability to selectively report or hide social media involvement. Direct observation of online activity has found that some adolescents encourage others to engage in antisocial talk; use social exclusion and harassment; and talk about somatic complaints, sexuality, and substance abuse.

The Internet provides new avenues to maintain social relationships with face-to-face friends as well as offers a new setting to meet new friends. It has changed how and how often we communicate with others. The Internet provides many positive opportunities for friendships, but it also affords new areas of risk.

33. Is technology bad for friendship? How can the Internet be helpful for friendship?

Research about online friendships is beginning to emerge. It has primarily worked to answer three questions: Do adolescents and young adults engage with peers similarly on social media platforms as they do in offline social interactions? How does engagement with social media relate to qualities of relationships? And how do peer interactions via social media relate to adolescents' and young adults' psychological adjustment? (See Question 31—Is having a friend online the same as having a friend in person for exploration of the first two topics?) This entry will focus on how online communication impacts psychological adjustment.

Trying to understand how engagement with peers on social media is related to psychological adjustment is challenging because social media includes so many different activities (e.g., creating a profile, posting status updates, managing connections, viewing and responding to others' activities, communicating by private message). Research on adults has indicated that intense engagement with Facebook might be related to poor psychological health. Five types of stress related to Facebook usage have been found: lack of privacy, exposure to irritating content, relationship conflict, social comparison, and jealousy. However, it is possible that adolescents engage with social media differently than adults, which might differentially impact their psychological adjustment. Few studies have examined specifically how posting online relates to emotional adjustment, but results from experimental studies with college students suggest that posting on social media sites may be associated with positive psychological health. College students focusing on their own Facebook page was associated with positive self-views. The impact might differ by sex. Specifically, a study with adolescents found that active Facebook use was associated with depression for boys only. Similarly, another study of 13-year-olds found that engagement with multiple social networking sites was associated with cyberbullying and sharing passwords with friends. Increased checking of Facebook has been associated not only with high levels of emotional difficulties but also with feelings of connectedness and fitting in with the peer group. Among high school students, text messaging that included negative talk about others predicted internalizing (e.g., anxiety, depression) symptoms, text messaging with antisocial content predicted growth in rule-breaking behavior and aggression across the year, and text messaging about sex predicted increased sexual activity and increase in borderline personality features.

Posting and commenting on social media might also follow the rich-get-richer hypothesis. Youth who are socially competent and have many positive peer connections are more likely to receive support and positive affirmation in response to their online posts compared to their peers who have more social difficulties and emotional problems. A study of 15-year-olds found that depressive symptoms were associated with using social media to seek feedback and engage in social comparison. These associations were strongest for girls and those lower in popularity with their peers. It is possible that the link between social media and adjustment may lie in differing motivations. In a sample of college students, posting Facebook updates negatively predicted social adjustment and positively predicted loneliness; however, this relationship did not hold for those who reported using Facebook in order to maintain relationships. College students who are more likely to engage in social comparison and were heavy Facebook users have been shown to have more negative affect and lower self-esteem after engaging in a short Facebook session compared to those lower in social comparison orientation. Similarly, college students who reported spending more time on Facebook perceived that others were happier and had better lives than they did. Further, when adolescents and young adults lurk online, they run the risk of seeing their friends engaging in social activities without them. Lurking tends to be difficult to study, but early research evidence suggests that passive Facebook use (viewing friends' profiles) was associated with depression in girls. A sample of 15-year-old students found that viewing pictures of friends drinking or smoking online was associated with increase in actual smoking and alcohol consumption. A large survey of adolescents has also found that intense engagement with social media predicted sleep disruptions, poorer sleep quality, and lower satisfaction with school. Social media usage also seems to impact attention and problem-solving skills. A study of college students found that using social media led to poorer task performance in a classroom simulation. Generally, research findings to date suggest that online interactions intensify features of social relationships and peer interactions that used to occur exclusively offline. The Internet enables adolescents to seek support at any time of day. Jealousy can also be exacerbated by social media and texting.

Research on Friendship

34. In what ways is friendship typically studied?

When you think about studying friendship, it may sound like a simple task: Can't you just ask someone who their friends are? However, it's actually quite a bit more complex than that. There are multiple dimensions of friendship that need to be assessed, and each of these is typically studied with a different approach. Generally, there are two major questions to answer—what to assess and how to measure it. When thinking about what to assess, there are five major domains of friendship experienced during adolescence: the presence of friendship, the quality of the relationship, characteristics of the friend, the context of the friendship, and the interactions with that friend. These five domains are not independent of one another, and most studies of friendship do not look at all of these aspects.

We will first take a look at how the presence of friendship is studied. Given that friendship is considered a reciprocal (both people feel the same way), dyadic relationship (between two people), studying the presence of friendship typically requires two steps. First, you ask an adolescent who their friends are and then you determine whether or not that individual also nominated the same individual as a friend. This type of methodology is typically conducted in schools where students have classmates (e.g., middle school, high school). The most common approach is to have adolescents nominate a number of grade mates (typically around three), who they view as their friends. Each child's/adolescent's nominations are compared, and nominations where both children/adolescents nominated one another (i.e., reciprocal nominations) are considered evidence of a mutual friendship. One variation of this procedure combines the nomination procedure with a rating scale technique. Early studies asked adolescents to name their five best friends in their grade. Then they were asked how much they like each student in their grade by rating them from 1 ("don't like") to 5 ("like very much, as a best friend"). Adolescents were considered close friends if at least one listed the other as a best friend and they gave one another a rating of at least 4. Researchers have also used rating scales without friendship nominations and identified friends as adolescents who give the other the highest liking rating. It seems that friendship nominations are likely the most precise, but both friendship nominations and rating scale techniques are appropriate ways to determine the presence of friendships. One limitation of these approaches is that limiting adolescents to friends within their grade at school may not capture all of their friendships since students often have friends outside of their school (e.g., from sports teams, religious organizations, etc.).

During the 1980s, researchers became interested in children's and adolescents' perceptions of their own friendships. Psychologists were interested in learning what was different about friendships from other relationships. These were the first attempts to understand friendship quality. Friendship quality tells us that some relationships are better than others, and more positive features of friendship are generally associated with a higher quality relationship. During the next decade, several measures were developed in an effort to study friendship quality. Each of these measures will be briefly discussed here. Berndt and colleagues developed Berndt's Friendship Interview. For this measure, children and adolescents respond to a structured interview followed by open-ended interview questions. The questions focus on six aspects of friendship—play/association (e.g., companionship, spending time together), prosocial behavior (e.g., sharing and helping), intimacy (e.g., self-disclosure), loyalty (e.g., dependability), attachment and self-esteem enhancement (e.g., closeness and encouragement), and conflict (e.g., fighting/arguing). Five questions were included for each dimension. Children and adolescents were first asked if each of these things happened in their friendship and then how often they happened.

A very common measure of friendship quality used during adolescence is the Network of Relationships Inventory (NRI). This measure contains 30 items with three items tapping each of the seven social provisions— reliable alliance, nurturance, affection, admiration, instrumental help, companionship, and intimacy, and each of three additional relationship features—relative power, conflict, and antagonism. Adolescents respond on a 1 (little to none) to 5 (the most) scale, and it has been used during both adolescence and young adulthood.

Another widely used measure of friendship quality is the Friendship Qualities Scale (FQS). The FQS contains 23 items grouped into five broad subscales: companionship, conflict, help, security, and closeness. This measure is designed to be used with a best friend. Similarly, the Friendship Quality Questionnaire (FQQ) has been used with both adolescents and young adults. The FQQ assesses six dimensions of friendship quality—validation and caring, intimate exchange, companionship and recreation, help and guidance, conflict and betrayal, and conflict resolution. The measure is completed for a specific friend whose name is typically inserted into each of the scale's items, and adolescents respond on a 0 (not at all true) to 4 (really true) scale.

A measure designed to be used with older adolescents is the McGill Friendship Questionnaires. The first questionnaire looks at positive feelings toward a friend and the functions expected of a friend. It includes a subscale about positive feelings for a friend and another about satisfaction with the friendship. The second questionnaire assesses a friendship's functions—companionship, help, reliable alliance, self-validation, and emotional security. A nine-point scale is used to indicate how often a friend fulfills each of these functions.

Next, we'll take a brief look at how characteristics of friends are studied. This helps us understand what an adolescent or young adult's friends are like. There are two general ways to assess the characteristics of friends. First, you can ask questions about what an individual's friends are like, such as how many of your friends (e.g., none, some, many, all) smoke cigarettes? How many of your friends drink alcohol? Or researchers can ask participants to name their best friend and then respond to questions about that person's behavior. This area of friendship is much less commonly studied than the quality of friendships.

The context of the friendship is another important aspect of the relationship. Some aspects of context that may be examined by researchers include the larger social network in which the friendship is embedded, the level of acceptance or rejection experienced within the larger peer group, other support systems (such as family), and the cultural context. These contextual aspects may impact friendships and are thus important to study.

The final dimension to take a look at when studying friendship is the interactions between friends. This aspect of friendship is often considered dependent on other variables (e.g., gender, popularity, level of aggressiveness, level of social withdrawal). Interactions with friends have been studied using direct observation, interviews, questionnaires, and reports by teacher or parent. Relationship properties such as equality, closeness, loyalty, similarity, dominance, and mutual liking have all been assessed. Findings have indicated that differences between friends and nonfriends are greatest when the measures include self-report. This may mean that friends overestimate these characteristics within their friendships or that researchers are not very good at observing these intimate characteristics within friendships.

35. How is social acceptance/peer group acceptance studied?

Social acceptance or peer group acceptance is the degree to which an individual is liked or disliked by members of the peer group. Peer group acceptance is typically studied using something called sociometric techniques. The goal of sociometric techniques is to differentiate among children and adolescents who have different social roles in their peer group. As you might expect, these techniques are used when there is a defined peer group. As such, they are best utilized during middle and high school (or with younger children) rather than during adulthood.

Peer group acceptance during adolescence has most often been assessed using nomination procedures. With most of these tools, adolescents are asked to nominate classmates (typically up to three or four classmates) who fit various relational criteria (e.g., peers you most like to spend time with). In one approach, nominations were then divided into positive and negative nominations to create two status dimensions: "social impact" (sum of positive and negative nominations received) and "social preference" (number of positive nominations minus the number of negative nominations). This approach was not very widely accepted, and a new approach was created. In this method, a "standard score" is created where positive nominations received are summed and then standardized to create a "liked most" score, and then the negative nominations received are summed and then standardized to create a "liked least" score. These two scores are then added together to arrive at a "social impact" score and then subtracted from one another to arrive at a "social preference" score. Finally, these two scores are used to classify adolescents into one of five peer status categories: popular peer status (high social preference scores, many positive nominations, and few negative nominations), rejected peer status (low social preference scores, few positive nominations, many negative nominations), neglected peer status (low social impact scores, few positive nominations, and few negative nominations), controversial peer status (high social impact scores, both high positive and negative nominations), and average peer status (moderate social preference scores and near average social impact scores).

A similar method for assessing peer group acceptance has peers nominate both most and least liked peers, and then these are used to create five peer status groups: populars, rejects, neglects, controversials, and averages. Peers are asked to make three positive and three negative nominations, and then probability theory is used to assign peers to each of the five status groups. This method was used less frequently than the peer nomination procedure described previously.

Using sociometric techniques, researchers have found that adolescent peer status is more stable than peer status during childhood. The rejected peer status is also the most stable over time, particularly during adolescence, but also during childhood as well. Researchers have examined the behavior of adolescents who are part of each peer status group. One way that behavior has been studied is to look at how peers attempt to enter a group. This is a challenging task for all individuals, but differences between the peer status groups have been found. Those who are popular have been found to exhibit more relevant, group-oriented tactics to enter a group. Those who are rejected by their peers tend to use more disruptive entry tactics, and those who are neglected by their peers tend to be more likely to wait or hover in the proximity of the peer group without speaking or trying to actively enter.

Since adolescents' peer group tends to expand as they make friends outside of school, popularity has also been assessed using an adolescent's own sense of social acceptance. An individual's own sense of social acceptance may become an increasingly popular marker of social success as they get older. One study that examined teens' perceived social acceptance found that teens who felt socially confident and comfortable with their peers did well regardless of their actual social status. Similarly, teens who were highly preferred by their peers, regardless of their own perceptions, also did well socially. The teens who did the worst were those who were unpopular with their peers and lacked a strong sense of their own social acceptance.

36. What does research tell us about helping those who struggle with friendship?

We have discussed that friendship is important for psychological well-being, so what does this mean about those who struggle to make friends?

How can we help them? I will provide a brief review of some of the interventions that have attempted to assist those who have difficulty making friends. If friendship interventions are successful, they may lead to better academics; smoother school transitions; better coping skills to deal with stress; lower levels of symptoms of loneliness, anxiety, and depression; and a lower likelihood of being bullied by peers. They may also help better prepare adolescents for romantic relationships and help individuals to feel happier and more satisfied with their lives.

The first wave of interventions aimed at improving the social lives of children and adolescents focused on improving peer relationships, rather than improving friendships. Specifically, they focused on improving peer acceptance and reducing peer rejection. Three major types of intervention have attempted to improve peer acceptance: social skills training programs, social-cognitive programs, and peer-pairing interventions. Social skills training programs focus on improving social competencies, such as social knowledge, social skills, and skill monitoring, with the goal that this will improve children's and adolescents' behavior with peers and lead to improved peer relations. The majority of social skills training programs were developed during the 1970s and 1980s. Results of these studies indicated that peer status and behavior do improve significantly as a result of the intervention programs. Changes in social behavior were noted more frequently than changes in peer status. There have been a few studies that have specifically examined how social skills training impacts friendship. One study in the late 1970s targeted children with low peer acceptance, taught them social skills related to playing individually with a peer in one-on-one coaching sessions, provided opportunities for practicing these skills in play sessions with another classmate, and then reviewed the play session with their coach. Results indicated that there were small improvements in best friend nominations for children in the coaching group. Some children went from having none to having one friend. Another study from the 1990s was designed to teach skills for social interaction with both the larger peer group and in dyadic friendships. The program worked directly with children on their social skills and included a significant parent component. Results found that boys who participated in the intervention improved their social skills, but whether or not they gained friends was not directly examined in the study. A more recent social skills program called S.S. Grin aims to improve peer relationships, and friendship indirectly, in children with a variety of peer problems (i.e., peer rejection, peer victimization/bullying, social anxiety). This program has been implemented in school settings. Results showed that children who received social skills training weekly over an eight-week period showed improvement in being liked, self-esteem, self-efficacy, and social anxiety. They also showed a decrease in affiliations with antisocial peers.

Social skills training has also been a component of more comprehensive intervention programs. One example is the "friendship group" component of the Fast Track prevention program. The Fast Track program was begun in the 1990s to prevent serious conduct problems in adolescence. High-risk children are identified by the end of their kindergarten year, and the program lasts from first grade through tenth grade. The program addresses both child (e.g., social skills, academic competency, self-regulation) and parent and family needs (e.g., discipline, parental response to conflict and frustration). The program also works to promote communication between home and school. The social skills component uses friendship groups to teach skills that are developmentally appropriate for establishing and maintaining friendship. The intervention includes lessons provided by teachers, small group instruction, role-play, discussion, and modeling. Children are provided with a "peer pair" in their classroom, and their interactions are observed. Results of the friendship group component of the Fast Track program have found that at the end of first grade, observations of the students in their classrooms and on the playground showed higher levels of positive exchanges with peers and higher social preference scores based on sociometric nominations by their peers. Moreover, positive behavior in the friendship groups was associated with improvement in problem-solving, emotion recognition, prosocial behavior, and positive peer interactions and a decrease in hostile attributions (attributing ambiguous situations to hostile intent) and aggressive and disruptive behaviors Unfortunately, the improvement in social status did not continue to be found at the end of third grade. But at the end of fourth grade, there were a number of significant improvements in peer relations, including higher peer acceptance and less peer rejection, fewer substance abusing peers, and greater teacher-rated social competence.

The second area of intervention focus is social-cognitive skills. Social cognition focuses on the underlying cognitive processes that facilitate or interfere with successful peer relationships. This can include several dimensions: thoughts about the self and others; thoughts about relationships between people; and thoughts about social groups, rules, and roles. As such, social-cognitive skills include perspective-taking, social problem-solving, conflict management, and social goals. The Anger Coping program/Coping Power program was developed for aggressive boys. Results indicated that aggression decreased and time on task increased, which led to higher perceived social competence. These gains were maintained over a three-year period. Similarly, a 15-month intervention focused on peer relations with aggressive and disruptive boys in fourth and fifth grades. The child component included group sessions focused on peer problems and lessons on perspective-taking, attribution-retraining (to reduce the hostile attribution bias), social problem-solving skills; skills in avoiding peer pressure; and relaxation techniques for handling anger. Results indicated that social-cognitive intervention can be effective. Across the middle school transition, the Coping Power program has led to improved social skills, social behavior, and social problem-solving skills. More recently, the Social Cognitive Intervention Program (SCIP) was developed to help 8–13-year old children diagnosed with oppositional defiant disorder and conduct disorder with the goal of changing social cognitive deficits and distortions in social information-processing. Children were randomly assigned to SCIP, social skills training, or a wait-list control. In the social skills group, children learned how to join a group, how to negotiate, and how to be helpful and supportive of their peers. Results indicated that SCIP and social skills training were both effective at post-treatment and one-year follow-up. They showed significant improvement in aggressive and disruptive behavior, self-control, social-cognitive skills, and appropriate social skills and social behavior.

The final approach to improving peer relationships are the peer-pairing interventions. These approaches work at the dyadic level with the goal of creating an ongoing close relationship. Some of the earliest work in this area was completed in the 1970s and 1980s on pair therapy. Two children, typically in pre- or early adolescence with contrasting but equally ineffective approaches to friendship, come together. They meet regularly with a therapist with the goal of using peer conflict in a therapeutic way to understand and teach conflict management skills. The goal is to increase both intimacy and autonomy by first improving social knowledge, social skills, and social values. The benefits of pair therapy are largely derived from clinical notes and case studies rather than research studies, and they indicate some positive outcomes, such as increased awareness of skills needed to interact with friends. Qualitative reports have found increase in negotiation, quality of communication, interpersonal understanding of friendship, and knowledge of strategies to deal with friendship dilemmas. Another peer-pairing approach is the buddy system for children with attention deficit hyperactivity disorder (ADHD). Children with ADHD tend to have significant problems with peer relationships and friendship. Children are paired with a buddy during the third week of an eight-week intervention program. They spend the most time with their buddy compared to other peers and are encouraged to share with their buddy. Parents were also encouraged to get the peers together to play on a weekly basis. Findings indicated that the quality of friendship was predicted by the number of times parents arranged for the children to get together.

Finally, individual and group therapy approaches have also been used to help improve peer difficulties. They may target social skills or social-cognitive skills. One group therapy intervention worked to improve intimacy with a close friend during 15 weekly classroom-based group therapy sessions. These sessions focused on developing language for feelings, improving self-acceptance and self-awareness, discussing perceptions about friendship, discussing difficulties in establishing and maintaining friendships, and talking about fears about close relationships. Adolescents in the intervention group reported an increase in intimacy with their best friend up to six months later.

❖

Case Studies

1. TRACY MOVES TO A NEW STATE

Tracy is a 14-year-old girl who is about to start her freshman year of high school. She grew up in a suburb of Chicago, where she has lived her whole life with her mother, father, and eight-year-old brother. Tracy's mother recently took a new job in New York City, which required her family to relocate. Tracy was really upset when her parents told her that they would have to move. She was really concerned about leaving behind all of her friends and the only place she has ever lived. Tracy was already feeling nervous about starting at a bigger high school, and now not only does she have to start high school but she also has to do so in a completely different place where she knows no one. Tracy's parents reassured her that she will do great meeting new friends and that they can come back to see her old friends at least twice a year when they go to visit Tracy's grandparents.

Tracy broke the bad news about her move to her small group of best girlfriends. They were all sad to hear that Tracy had to move, but they reassured her that they would all keep in touch and remain friends. Tracy's friends threw her a going-away party at her favorite local restaurant. They made her feel really special, and they all had a great time. Tracy and her friends also made a clear plan of how they would all keep in touch. They decided that they would send letters in the mail at least once a month, text every day, and talk over video chat at least once a week. Although Tracy was still nervous and sad about leaving her friends behind, she felt a little bit better that they seemed so enthusiastic and committed to keeping in touch with her.

Over the summer, Tracy and her family settled into their new house in the suburbs of New York City. She had played soccer her whole life, so her parents found her a summer soccer team that she could play on as soon as they moved. Through soccer, Tracy met a few other girls, whom she connected with and who were also going to go to the same high school. These girls invited Tracy to go to movies and go bowling. Tracy began to feel a little bit better about starting at her new school since she at least now knew a couple of people. Tracy got her schedule and talked to her new friends. She was thrilled to find out that she had a couple of classes with her new friends, and they assured her that they would introduce her to lots of people.

The week before school started, Tracy became really nervous about what was to come. She tried talking to her family, but her brother only said, "What's the big deal? It's cool that we get to live right by New York City and meet new people." Tracy didn't think her brother or her parents had any idea what she was going through. All summer, Tracy's friends from back home kept their promises of keeping in touch. The week before school started, they all did a video chat during which Tracy shared her concerns about her new school. She was a little relieved to find out that her friends were feeling a really similar way with their transition to the high school.

The first few weeks of school were really hard. Tracy felt out of place and like she'd never find her groove. The girls from her soccer team were nice, but Tracy still had five classes where she didn't really know anyone. Once school started, Tracy's friends from back home were a little less available and not as good about keeping in touch as regularly. Tracy joined the school soccer team where she met a few more friends. After the first month or two of school, Tracy started to feel more settled. She had made a few close friends and was settling into her new school routine. By the end of the first year at her new school, Tracy had a new close group of good girlfriends and did well academically. She still keeps in touch with her friends back in Illinois. Although they don't talk as frequently as they once did, they still text each other about once a week and video chat monthly. Tracy thought the move was the most difficult thing she had ever done; however, she felt like it helped her to be more prepared for when she would go off to college in a few years.

Analysis

As you can see, Tracy fared quite well during her move and subsequent adjustment to her new school. Some of the protective factors for Tracy were that she had a strong supportive family, a high level of social competence, and a good group of supportive friends. Tracy experienced some really common emotions during this transition. She felt nervous, scared, and sad to leave behind her old home and friends. At times, Tracy felt like no one understood how she was feeling, most especially her family. However, many things that Tracy and her family did helped to ease her transition and make it as smooth as possible. Tracy set up a plan for keeping in touch with her friends; she got involved with a new activity right away in her new town where she had the potential to make new friends, and she remained in contact with her old friends. Joining the summer soccer league and the fall soccer team at school proved really helpful for Tracy's adjustment. Even though Tracy had many protective factors to help ease her adjustment and make it as smooth as possible, she still found the first year in her new school to be her most challenging year ever. Importantly, the middle school and high school years are some of the most challenging times for a move due to all the significant changes that are taking place during puberty and adolescence physically, socially, and emotionally. Although Tracy's contact with her friends back in Illinois decreased somewhat as she made new social connections and they all started high school, maintaining contact with those friends likely helped Tracy to feel less alone and adjust to her new home and school.

2. JOSEPH IS HAVING TROUBLE MAKING FRIENDS IN COLLEGE

Joseph is a 20-year-old sophomore in college who is majoring in audio engineering. He attended school approximately two hours from his family's home. According to Joseph's mother, he had always been a shy, reserved kid who kept to himself. He never had very many friends. When he was younger, he preferred to build things and put together puzzles more than playing with other children. In middle school and high school, Joseph was known as the kid who always had headphones on and was listening to music. He was never popular with his peers. Joseph always did well in school up until his second semester of college; however, his grades have gradually declined since then.

Joseph chose his college because they had his major of choice. He was initially really looking forward to his classes, but like he had in the past, he struggled to make friends after he transitioned to college. Joseph's randomly assigned roommate moved out after his first semester freshman year. His roommate didn't tell him why he changed roommates, but Joseph never really talked to him. He now has a single dorm room. Joseph usually attends his classes, but he has struggled to attend his 8:00 a.m. classes lately. Beginning in the second semester of his freshman year, once he lived alone, Joseph started to turn to alcohol to cope with the anxiety he felt when interacting with his peers. It started out with just a beer or two here and there, but it quickly escalated to drinking at least a six pack a day. When he'd return from class in the afternoon, he'd usually drink alone, and this is what started making it hard for him to wake up for his early classes.

Joseph's parents were concerned about the decline in his grades, but he assured them that everything was fine. They didn't know that he drank as he never drank in high school. He said that his coursework was just getting more challenging, but that he was going to buckle down this semester and turn his grade point average around. His parents encouraged him to study with someone else from the audio engineering program or to go to the tutoring center. He assured them that he would do one of those things and that everything was going to be fine.

Joseph had always been true to his word, so he worked up the courage to talk to another guy who had been in a bunch of his classes, Tom. He asked Tom if he might be able to help him study for the midterm in their class. Tom said sure, and they started to study together a few times per week, and they sometimes studied with a group of students from their major. This got Joseph out of his dorm room more and interacting with others for the first time in a long time. He also started to cut down some on his drinking since he was spending more time studying with others. Joseph started to get to know Tom better, and Tom asked him to play pool. Joseph thought that Tom was really nice and relaxed, and he felt more and more comfortable around him over time. He had a lot of fun playing pool with him, and they started to hang out more regularly. Joseph got his midterms again, and he got all Bs and an A. He was really happy, and his parents were thrilled that academics seemed to be looking up for him.

Tom introduced Joseph to some of his other friends. Although Joseph was initially nervous around these new people, he started to get to know them and gradually became more comfortable. Joseph finished out the second semester of his sophomore year by making the dean's list. He also now had a close group of friends with whom he spent time nearly every day. Joseph still drank, but now he only had a drink or two when he was with other people. He never drank alone. Joseph's parents were really proud of him. He planned to live with Tom and one of their other buddies next year. For the first time ever, Joseph was actually a little bit bummed about going home for the summer since he'd be away from his friends for a couple of months. He and Tom have planned to meet up in a city between where they both live to go to a concert.

Analysis

Joseph's story is not an unusual one for a socially withdrawn, introverted individual. When he was young, he preferred objects over people, generally kept to himself, and had difficulty making friends. Often, although socially withdrawn youth are interested in their peers, their anxiousness about interacting tends to keep them from doing so. Like other socially withdrawn children and adolescents, Joseph was not well accepted by his peer group. Joseph's peer difficulties continued when he went off to college. His roommate moved out after the first semester, and Joseph turned to alcohol to cope with his social struggles. He began to see a decline in his grades. Using alcohol or drugs to cope is not unusual during adolescence and young adulthood.

Fortunately for Joseph, he connected with another guy in his major. They first started studying together but then began to hang out socially. This guy introduced him to other friends. Forming even this one close friendship was a strong protective factor for Joseph as even having one close reciprocated friendship can contribute to psychological well-being. In Joseph's case, it also helped him to decrease his drinking and improve his academics.

3. SAM'S PARENTS GET A DIVORCE

Sam is a 16-year-old girl who lives in San Diego, California, with her mom and dad. Sam is an only child. She has a couple of cousins, an aunt and uncle, and her grandparents who also live in the next town over from her. She has always had close relationships with both her parents. Sam has lived in the same community since she was born. She has a close-knit group of girlfriends who have been friends with one another since kindergarten. Sam is a junior in high school and is getting ready to apply to colleges. She hopes to become a doctor one day. Sam is a good student who mostly gets As and is in honors classes. She particularly loves Biology, Chemistry, and English.

Everything had been going really well in Sam's life until she started noticing that her parents were fighting a lot more than they ever had in the past. They seemed to fight about money, who was doing more around the house, and how much time her dad was spending at work away from the family. Lately, it seemed like her parents were either fighting or not speaking to one another at all. After a really big blowup the week before, Sam's dad did not come home that night. Sam could not remember a single night in her whole life when both her parents had not been home.

She cried herself to sleep, worrying about what might happen, and she wondered if there was anything she could do to fix their relationship.

On Friday, when Sam got home from school, both her parents were sitting in the living room waiting for her. They asked her if the three of them could sit down and talk together. Sam's parents shared how much they both loved her and that she had not done anything wrong, but that they had decided to get a divorce. Sam was devastated. She never imagined that this was something that would happen to her family. Sam's dad shared that he had rented an apartment just a few blocks away (still within the same school district) and that Sam could come to his apartment anytime she wanted to do so. He also promised to still take her to visit colleges with her mom during spring break. Sam was so upset that she really couldn't say much of anything to her parents.

Sam ran to her room and cried into her pillow. She started to think of all the ways this might change her family and her future. Sam decided to call her friend Amelia. She thought Amelia might be able to understand what she was going through because her parents had got divorced when she was in eighth grade. Amelia told her that she was so sorry that Sam was going through this and that she knew how sad and upsetting it is. Amelia asked Sam to go to the movies and out for coffee to try to get her mind off everything that was happening. Sam agreed to do so. Amelia was a great listener. Sam shared all of the things she was concerned about and how surprised she was that her parents were doing this. Amelia just listened and offered advice only when she was asked to do so. Amelia shared that it was really hard the first few months after her parents' divorce and a really big adjustment, but that now there are actually some things she likes about it. Amelia said she gets to spend a lot more time with each of her parents doing fun things than she had ever done before. Sam said that she had no idea how she was going to tell all of their other friends, and Amelia offered to tell them with her.

Amelia gathered all of their close friends together at her house and helped Sam tell them all that her parents were going to get a divorce. All of Sam's friends quickly gave her hugs and said that they would be there to support her no matter what. The next day, two of Sam's friends dropped off homemade cookies to her and another friend sent flowers with a card. Each day, Sam's friends texted her or called her to make sure she was doing OK. As hard as this was, Sam was so grateful for her friends and really felt supported by them.

The first few weeks back at school were really hard for Sam. She had a hard time focusing in her classes and on her schoolwork and often cried herself to sleep at night. Sam didn't want to burden her mom with how she was feeling because she knew this was already really hard for her mom. Sam's dad called her nearly every day to talk to her, and she started spending weekends with him at his apartment where she had her own room. Sam's friends continued to be there for her. They checked in with her each day and invited her to do something most days to keep her busy and her mind off what was going on with her parents. After a few months, Sam felt like she had come to terms with what was happening, and things had mostly gone back to normal for her at school. She had gone on the college trip with her parents, and they actually seemed to get along pretty well. Mostly, Sam was just really grateful for her good friends who helped her get through the hardest thing she had ever faced.

Analysis

Sam is at the developmental stage of adolescence when her parents decide to get a divorce. This is a time of transition when adolescents begin to depend more upon their friends than their parents for emotional support, and also tend to spend increasing time with friends. Thus, it is not surprising that Sam turns to her close-knit group of friends when her parents tell her that they are getting a divorce. She is an only child and doesn't feel like she can turn to her parents about her own feelings. Sam does have some difficulty adjusting to this huge life change. She has difficulty focusing on schoolwork, feels lonelier, and cries more often. Fortunately, these symptoms tend to be fairly transient for Sam. Confiding in her friend whose parents had also gone through a divorce is really helpful for her. Her friends do just what good friends should do when something really stressful or hard happens to their friend. They are there to listen to her; they only offer advice when she asks for it, and they keep her busy by distracting her and asking her to do things often. Unfortunately, adolescents who do not have close friends when they go through something like their parents' divorce or other loss tend not to fare as well. They are more prone to developing symptoms of loneliness, anxiety, and depression or to act out (e.g., drinking, drug abuse, delinquent behavior).

4. JULIE HAS A RIFT IN HER FRIENDSHIP

Julie is a sophomore in high school. Her very best friend's name is Ellie, and they have been friends since kindergarten. They met on their very first day of kindergarten. At the time, they both loved My Little Pony and playing house. Although their interests have changed over the years, Julie and Ellie are still inseparable. The rest of their friend group has come and gone over the years, but Julie and Ellie have always remained close. During high school, they try to arrange their schedules so that they can have as many classes together as possible; they always eat lunch together, they both run track together, they see one another nearly every day, and they are always together on the weekends. Julie has always felt like she can tell Ellie anything and has never really kept any secrets from her. Ellie is always the first person Julie goes to if she's feeling nervous about something or when she thinks she likes a boy. Ellie has always been a great listener, can always be trusted with a secret, and is a great person to bounce ideas off too. Julie feels like she is this person for Ellie as well.

One day, after Julie and Ellie get out of their Spanish class, their last for the day, they decide to go over to Julie's house to hang out together. Ellie confides in Julie that she really likes this guy, Ben, who is a senior in their Spanish class. Julie tells her that he is cute but that she heard that he drinks quite a bit and smokes, both things that Ellie and Julie do not do. Ellie says that she just doesn't care. If she has any chance with Ben, she is definitely going to go for it. Julie goes on to tell Ellie that she's feeling nervous about her geometry test coming up next week. Julie is not even sure that Ellie heard what she is saying as she seems really distracted.

The next week at school, Julie watches Ellie and Ben carefully during Spanish class. She thinks she notices Ben checking Ellie out during class. Julie casually mentions this to Ellie after class, and Ellie just glows. It all seems to happen quickly, but by the next week, Ben asks Ellie if she'd like to go on a date with him. Ellie, of course, says yes. Julie goes over to Ellie's house to help her pick out her clothes and get ready. She also tells Ellie to be careful. Ellie has a lot of fun on her date, and she and Ben start spending a lot of time together. Julie thinks that Ellie seems so busy and consumed by her new relationship with Ben that she really doesn't have time for her anymore. Ellie starts sitting with Ben during lunch and barely responds to her text messages. When she does, she gives really short responses. They definitely don't see each other much outside of school, and Ellie is never available on the weekends anymore.

Julie's friendship with Ellis is really important to her. She understands that dating someone new is exciting and that Ellie will want to spend quite a bit of time with Ben, but she hopes that this doesn't destroy their friendship or make them grow apart. So, Julie decides she needs to sit down with Ellie and talk to her about her concerns. Ellie agrees to meet her for coffee. Julie makes sure to tell Ellie how she is feeling and not to make it all about what Ellie has done to her. "Ellie, I've been feeling like we may be starting to grow apart. I'm really excited for you and Ben, but I've been feeling pretty lonely and left out." Ellie tells Julie how sorry she is that she has been feeling left out and lonely and asks what she can do to make things better. She reassures Julie that she is her best friend and that she knows that she has been distracted lately. Julie and Ellie agree to get together, just the two of them, every other week. Ellie also promises to introduce Julie to Ben and his friends. She reassures Julie that they are actually really nice.

The next week, Julie and Ellie get together to watch movies and hang out together on Friday night. On Saturday, Ellie introduces Julie to Ben and his friends. They all hang out together, and Julie actually has a really good time. They all make plans to get together again the next week. Julie feels much better after she gets her feelings off her chest; she feels heard by Ellie and gets to meet these new people in Ellie's life. She feels like their friendship might just find a new normal.

Analysis

Julie and Ellie had been friends for many years. It is not unusual for high school students to begin dating, and this can have a significant impact on friendships. When Julie's best friend Ellie started dating an older guy, she began to feel lonely and left out. Fortunately for Julie, she did not keep these feelings to herself. She sat down with Ellie and discussed her concerns right away. She also used good communication skills when she focused on her feelings rather than saying everything that Ellie was doing wrong or to her. Ellie also did some really good things to show that she valued their friendship and wanted to work to maintain it. She continued to carve out time for just Julie, and she included Julie in get-togethers with her boyfriend and his friends. Although their friendship may not ever be exactly the same as it used to be, keeping open lines of communication, continuing to be there for one another, and including Julie in this new group are sure to go a long way in maintaining their friendship.

5. OLIVER'S WHOLE NEW WORLD OF FRIENDSHIP

Oliver is an 18-year-old Caucasian young man. He grew up in a very small town in rural Maine. Both of Oliver's parents have worked their whole lives in a factory, and Oliver is going to be the first person in his family to attend college. His parents are very proud of him and believe he's setting a great example for his younger sister. Oliver has lived in this small town his whole life. He has a close group of friends who are all quite similar to him. They are all white, and most of their parents also work in the local factory. As Oliver gets older, he realizes that he wants more for himself than this small town and working at the factory. He has dreams of becoming a doctor and worked really hard in high school so that he can move out of state to go to college. Oliver will be attending college in New York City this fall. He is really looking forward to expanding his horizons in a new big city and by meeting lots of new people from all over the world.

When Oliver arrives at school in the fall, he is excited to meet and get to know his roommate, Thomas, who has come all the way from France to attend college in New York. Oliver and Thomas get along pretty well and are really interested in learning about one another's cultures. Thomas cannot believe that Oliver comes from a town of only a few hundred people, as he assumes that most of America has big cities like New York. Oliver cannot imagine growing up in Paris, like Thomas has. They find that their eating and sleeping patterns are very different. Thomas is used to having a large meal mid-day and having dinner around 10:00 p.m. Oliver is used to having dinner with his family around 5:00 p.m. and waking up early to see his parents off to their jobs at the factory and helping with his younger sister. Oliver enjoys hearing about all of Thomas's travels as he has been all over the world. The new roommates also realize that they do have several things in common. They both enjoy playing and watching soccer (or futbol), running, and spending time with their friends. Once they begin classes, they each meet some other students and make some other friends. Oliver meets several other guys who have also come to New York from small towns. They also enjoy hunting and fishing like he does. Thomas meets a lot of other international students with whom he feels he has more in common as well.

Oliver and Thomas continue to spend some time together, mostly going for runs and watching soccer matches. However, they both begin to spend even more time with their other new groups of friends. Oliver, though, is still really interested in getting to know people who are different from him. So, Thomas invites him to spend more time with his group of international students so that he can get to know them. Oliver really enjoys learning all about their different cultures, customs, and different foods that they eat. He especially enjoys trying out restaurants around New York City that offer ethnic cuisine. Oliver also realizes that although he initially thought he'd have nothing in common with Thomas's friends, they actually have a lot in common. Many of them are in the same major (they also want to become doctors) and also grew up in small towns. The coolest part about getting to know Thomas is that Oliver gets to leave the country for the first time. Over spring break, Oliver joins Thomas for a trip back to Paris to meet his family. They also travel to Belgium and Germany.

As time goes on, with the exception of Thomas, Oliver generally spends most of his time with the original group of friends he met who are also from small towns across the United States and have similar hobbies. Thomas spends most of his time with other international students. However, Oliver and Thomas form a really solid bond and become really good friends. They open each other up to very different worlds they never knew they would experience. After the spring semester ends, Thomas actually makes a brief trip to Maine before returning to France for summer vacation.

Analysis

The story of Oliver and Thomas shows how people from very different backgrounds can become and stay friends. Oliver grew up in a small town in rural Maine, while Thomas grew up in Paris, France. They met when they became roommates during their freshman year of college. Oliver and Thomas built a relationship on things that they had in common (soccer, running), and they had a genuine interest and curiosity in learning more about one another and their differing cultures. Importantly, Oliver and Thomas met at a key time of transition in both of their lives. This helped enable them to form a strong friendship during their first year of college that they were able to continue over time. They solidified their friendship by traveling to one another's homes and meeting one another's families. Research has shown that friendships formed during the first year of college can transcend differences. However, you also saw that Oliver and Thomas both made a group of friends who were more similar to themselves. Although they worked to introduce one another to these friends, and they enjoyed getting to know one another, they both ultimately gravitated toward the group of friends who were most like them. This is not unusual to see. We tend to become friends with people who are similar to us with regard to race, ethnicity, and religion. However, the story of Oliver and Thomas shows you that it is possible to become friends with those who are different from us.

Glossary

Average acceptance: Adolescents or young adults who receive a moderate number of liked most nominations and few liked least nominations during sociometric techniques.

Clique: A group of adolescents, with shared interests or other features in common, who spend time together and do not readily allow others to join their group.

Companionship: One of the key provisions of friendship. It involves spending time with one another, which provides a feeling of friendship.

Controversial: Adolescents or young adults who receive many liked most nominations and many liked least nominations during sociometric techniques.

Co-rumination: Excessively and repeatedly discussing personal problems with a friend. There is mutual encouragement for discussing problems, speculating about them, and a focus on negative feelings. It is linked to both positive friendship adjustment and internalizing difficulties.

Dyadic relationship: In friendship, this refers to a close and reciprocal connection between two individuals.

Friendship: An interpersonal, dyadic, horizontal relationship between two individuals.

Friendship nomination procedure: The way in which the presence of friendship is typically studied. First, adolescents and young adults name who their friends are (typically within a grade or school). Nominations between the two individuals are compared, and if both individuals nominate one another, that is considered evidence of a mutual friendship.

Friendship quality: A high-quality friendship is characterized by high levels of prosocial behavior, intimacy, and other positive features and low levels of conflict, rivalry, and other negative friendship features.

Gossip: Discussing private information that someone shared with you behind their back. Typically involves telling secrets or other information that was asked to be kept private.

Intimacy: With regard to friendship, it refers to the closeness between two friends. It is a key provision of friendship that becomes increasingly important during adolescence and builds over time.

Neglected: Adolescents or young adults who receive few liked most nominations and also few liked least nominations during sociometric techniques.

Peer acceptance: The degree to which an adolescent or young adult is socially accepted by their peers. It is typically measured by the level of popularity (typically assessed by sociometric techniques) with peers.

Peer victimization: The experience of being a target of physical or relational aggression by peers.

Popular: Adolescents or young adults who receive many liked most nominations and few liked least nominations during sociometric techniques.

Rejected: Adolescents or young adults who receive few liked most nominations and many liked least nominations during sociometric techniques.

Relational aggression: A type of aggression in which harm is caused by damaging someone's relationships or social status. It may involve things such as teasing, spreading rumors, or gossiping.

Resilience: The ability to recover from difficulties. In the context of friendship, it is the ability to overcome relationship difficulties and not experience or recover from emotional difficulties.

Rich-get-richer hypothesis: The idea that individuals who are socially competent, outgoing, and have positive face-to-face relationships will benefit most from the Internet and social relationships over the Internet. This hypothesis has received support.

Social acceptance: How well-liked an individual is by their overall peer group. This is typically studied using sociometric techniques.

Social compensation hypothesis: The idea that individuals who are introverted, shy, or socially anxious might benefit most from using the Internet and social relationships over the Internet. This hypothesis has not received much research support.

Social skills: A central component of social competence. Typically measured by a specific set of skills, sociometric status, relationships, or functional outcomes.

Social skills training: Programs focused on improving social competencies, such as social knowledge, skills, and skill monitoring, with the goal that this behavior with peers will lead to improved peer relations.

Social withdrawal: Individuals who frequently refrain from social activities in the presence of their peers. Lack of social interaction may result from social fear and anxiety or a preference for solitude. It is concurrently and predicatively associated with a range of negative outcomes (internalizing problems, peer difficulties, school difficulties).

Sociometric techniques: Methods that qualitatively measure aspects of social relationships, such as social acceptance (how much an individual is liked by peers) and social status (social standing in comparison to peers).

Directory of Resources

BOOKS

Bagwell, C.L., & Schmidt, M.E. (2011). *Friendships in Childhood & Adolescence*. The Guilford Press.

Bukowski, W.M., Laursen, B., & Rubin, K.H. (Eds.) (2018). *Handbook of Peer Interactions, Relationships, and Groups, Second Edition*. The Guildford Press.

Chen, X., French, D.C., & Schneider, B.H. (Eds.) (2006). *Peer Relationships in Cultural Context*. Cambridge University Press.

Kupersmidt, J.B., & Dodge, K.A. (Eds.) (2004). *Children's Peer Relations: From Development to Intervention*. American Psychological Association.

Ladd, G.W. (2005). *Children's Peer Relations and Social Competence: A Century of Progress*. Yale University Press.

Prinstein, M.J., & Dodge, K.A. (Eds.) (2008). *Understanding Peer Influence in Children and Adolescents*. The Guilford Press.

WEBSITES

https://www.parentingscience.com/social-skills-activities.html
This website provides examples of activities for developing social skills throughout the life span.

https://www.copingpower.com/
   This website provides information and resources about the Coping
   Power social-cognitive skills intervention program that was discussed
   in Question 36.

https://www.hhs.gov/ash/oah/adolescent-development/healthy-relationships
/healthy-friendships/index.html
   The United States Department of Health and Human Services website
   provides information on healthy friendship during adolescence. This
   site also provides information on healthy dating relationships and bullying during adolescence as well.

https://www.healthychildren.org/English/ages-stages/teen/school/Pages
/Making-Friends-in-High-School.aspx
   The American Academy of Pediatrics provides advice on how to make
   friends during high school. They also provide information about dating
   and substance abuse.

https://www.girlshealth.gov/relationships/friendships/
   The United States Department of Health and Human Services provides a website dedicated to women's and girl's health. This site
   provides information about true friendship, handling peer pressure,
   coping with cliques, how to handle fights with a friend, and when to
   end a friendship.

https://youngmenshealthsite.org/guides/friendship/
   Boston Children's Hospital's Division of Adolescent and Young Adult
   Medicine provides a Young Men's Health website dedicated to providing carefully researched health information to teenage boys and young
   men. They provide a brief guide to friendship during this time in life.

https://youngwomenshealth.org/2013/05/23/tween-friendship/
https://youngwomenshealth.org/2012/05/09/friendship/
   Boston Children's Hospital's Division of Adolescent and Young
   Adult Medicine and the Division of Gynecology provides a Young
   Women's Health website dedicated to providing carefully researched
   health information to teenage girls and young women. They provide
   a brief guide to friendship for "tween girls" and friendship during this
   time in life.

https://www.jhsph.edu/research/centers-and-institutes/center-for
-adolescent-health/_docs/TTYE-Guide.pdf
   The John Hopkins University Center for Adolescent Health produced
   a guide to healthy adolescent development. It includes information on
   bullying and emotional health.

https://www.hhs.gov/ash/oah/adolescent-development/healthy-
relationships/healthy-friendships/peer-pressure/index.html
   The United States Department of Health and Human Services provides information on peer pressure and suggestions for how adolescents
   can handle peer pressure.

https://www.aacap.org/AACAP/Families_and_Youth/Facts_for_Families
/FFF-Guide/Peer-Pressure-104.aspx
   The American Academy of Child and Adolescent Psychiatry provides
   information about peer pressure and how adolescents can handle peer
   pressure.

https://teenshealth.org/en/teens/expert/friends?ref=search
https://kidshealth.org/en/teens/peer-pressure.html
   Nemours, a nonprofit children's health system, provides a teen health
   website with information and resources for adolescents. They provide
   information about common questions that adolescents have about
   friendship and peer pressure.

https://www.stopbullying.gov/
   The United States federal government has developed a website on bullying that is managed by the Department of Health and Human Services. This website provides information on bullying and cyberbullying
   as well as prevention resources.

http://www.thebullyproject.com/
   The Bully Project is a social action campaign inspired by the film *Bully*.
   The website provides a toolkit and resources to help end bullying.

https://www.nasponline.org/resources-and-publications/resources
-and-podcasts/school-climate-safety-and-crisis/school-violence
-resources/bullying-prevention
   The National Association of School Psychologists provides resources
   to prevent bullying in schools.

https://socialpronow.com/blog/make-friends-online/
This website provides information about how to make friends online. It provides tips, websites, and app recommendations and highlights common mistakes that people make when trying to form new friendships.

HOTLINES

If you or someone you know is considering suicide, this hotline is available 24 hours per day:
National Suicide Prevention Lifeline (1-800-273-8255)

If you or someone you know is experiencing intimate partner violence, this hotline is available 24 hours per day:
National Domestic Violence Hotline 1-800-799-SAFE (7233)

If you or someone you know is struggling with drinking or drugs, this hotline is available 24 hours per day:
National Substance Abuse and Mental Health Services Hotline 1-800-662-HELP (4357)

Index

About the Author

Lauren Holleb, PhD, is an associate professor of psychology at Husson University and a licensed psychologist in part-time private practice. She is a Parent-Child Interaction Therapy (PCIT) International Certified Therapist who provides therapeutic services to children and their families, psychological evaluations for young children, and clinical supervision to graduate trainees. She received her PhD in developmental-clinical psychology from the University of Maine, completed her predoctoral internship at the University of Texas at Austin/Dell Children's Medical Center/Texas Child Study Center, and completed her postdoctoral fellowship at Cincinnati Children's Hospital Medical Center. Her published works include journal articles and book chapters on peer relationships, social skills, and social development.